The Bilingual Counselor's Guide to Spanish

Designed specifically with mental health professionals in mind, *The Bilingual Counselor's Guide to Spanish* is perfect for counselors interested in expanding their client base and language skill set. Featuring terminology and cultural phrases specific to the mental health profession, this text offers an easy introduction to both the Spanish language and interfacing with Spanish-speaking clients in a counseling setting. Sections of useful and practical vocabulary are followed by *¡Practique!* sections, which enable the reader to put his or her developing skills to use. These sections are augmented by case studies in English and Spanish, as well as brief overviews of Latino history, customs, and social manners that will greatly enhance any counselor's depth of interaction with Spanish-speaking clients. For counselors who want to communicate with the large and rapidly expanding population of Spanish speakers in the United States, or for those who are simply interested in developing or improving their Spanish-language skills, *The Bilingual Counselor's Guide to Spanish* is the place to start.

Roberto Swazo, PhD, is an associate professor and coordinator of the counselor education program at Florida Agricultural and Mechanical University in Tallahassee, Florida. In addition to teaching, Dr. Swazo is a frequent speaker at professional conferences, and conducts workshops throughout the United States and abroad on multicultural issues and psychobilingual training for schools and mental health agencies. He is the author of *Fantasías e ilusiones desde el exilio* (*Fantasies and Illusions from the Exile*) and co-author of *Assessment and Intervention with Children and Adolescents: Developmental and Multicultural Approaches*.

The Bilingual Counselor's Guide to Spanish

Basic Vocabulary and Interventions for the Non-Spanish Speaker

Roberto Swazo

Routledge
Taylor & Francis Group

NEW YORK AND LONDON

First published 2013
by Routledge
711 Third Avenue, New York, NY 10017

Simultaneously published in the UK
by Routledge
27 Church Road, Hove, East Sussex BN3 2FA

Routledge is an imprint of the Taylor & Francis Group, an informa business

Library of Congress Cataloging in Publication Data
Swazo, Roberto.
    The bilingual counselor's guide to Spanish :
    basic vocabulary and interventions for the non-Spanish speaker /
    Roberto Swazo.—1 Edition.
    pages cm
    Includes bibliographical references and index.
    1. Cross-cultural counseling. 2. Social workers—United States.
    3. Latin Americans—Services for—United States. I. Title.
    BF636.7.C76S93 2013
    361'.0608968073—dc23
    2012042653

ISBN: 978–0–415–81022–7 (hbk)
ISBN: 978–0–415–69907–5 (pbk)
ISBN: 978–0–203–13638–6 (ebk)

Typeset in Minion
by Swales & Willis Ltd, Exeter, Devon

To Dagmar, for her patience, relentless support, and unconditional understanding.

Todah Rabah HaShem.

Contents

Acknowledgements   ix
Introduction   xi

1   Who Are the Latinos/Hispanics?: A Brief Historical Overview of
    Their Culture and People   1

2   Cultural Norms and Family Systems: Considerations in the
    Latino/Hispanic Culture   13

3   An Introduction to and Review of the Spanish Language   19

4   Counselors, Social Workers, and Psychologists   45

5   Interventions for School Counselors and School Psychologists   93

6   Substance Abuse Professionals   125

7   Developing Spanish Bilingual Materials and Techniques on
    How to Work with an Interpreter   169

References   187
Index   193

Acknowledgements

I would like to thank Routledge for accepting this publication, Anna Moore, and in particular Sam Rosenthal, for his support, assistance, and encouragement. I appreciate the assistance of my graduate assistants, Liz Rosinski at Roosevelt University and the following counseling students from Roosevelt University: Daniel Vishny, Jessica López, Sara Pelaez, Rocío Zapata, Amanda Brullo, Jaymina Patel, Pamela Smith, Heather Lane, Philip Montgomery, and Candyce Jupiter. Also, I would like to thank Iga Celinska for all the technical assistance and expertise provided during the recording process.

Finally, thanks to all the graduate students, clinicians in the field, clients in general, and Spanish-speaking clients who encourage us to keep learning, researching, and developing the counseling and human services fields.

Introduction

Prologue

Mr. Jones, the high school principal seemed puzzled as he was about to call the cops on the distressed father. In a desperate attempt to grab the attention of Mr. Jones, the father of one of his students uttered: "¡Mi hijo se quiere matar, ayúdeme por favor!" In a vague recollection of his college Spanish courses, Mr. Jones recognizes the word "matar" (kill). Since the parent appeared to be highly distressed, Mr. Jones assumed that he was attempting to kill him. Fortunately, the assistant principal called the school counselor who knew some basic Spanish interventions and recognized the desperate claims of the parent: "My son wants to kill himself!" Immediately the school counselors said to the distressed father: "¡Yo le ayudaré! (I will help you). The dislocated face of the father changed completely and his eyes looked bright full of hope as he showed a weak smile to the school counselor.

This situation demonstrates how the basic knowledge of a language can help practitioners connect more effectively with monolingual Spanish-speaking Latino clients. The "culturally encapsulated" counselor is the epitome of the past, there is no longer room for mental health professionals who insist in providing services to clients who look, think, and speak like them. These multicultural and multilingual societies are here to stay and will keep evolving as we speak. Perhaps many mental health providers will not have such dramatic encounters but it is certain that they can help future clients to have a positive experience with the mental health environment. The acquisition of some basic Spanish skills can impact their Latino/Hispanic clients in ways that monolingual English-speaking professionals cannot.

Introduction

¡Hola! ¿Cómo estás? How many times have you faced a client or prospective Spanish-speaking client and have not been able to say absolutely anything? You essentially froze. How many times have you wondered if you could use some of those basic Spanish skills that you learned in high school and/or college? Or perhaps, even if you have not taken Spanish classes before, would you like to at least know how to direct or refer a client to the right professional, agency, or counselor? This is the time to start!

This book is intended to provide basic interactive Spanish skills for counseling practitioners (i.e., mental health, community, substance abuse, school counseling), psychology, and social workers who have limited knowledge of the Spanish language and Latino culture. It can also be a guide for those of you who have a basic knowledge of the language but do not know how to use the correct terminology in a counseling context. In addition, the book provides a wealth of cultural information, vocabulary, and cultural terms that can assist a mental health clinician in determining a diagnosis or an intervention during the therapy process. Fluency and conversational skills in Spanish require a deeper knowledge of the language and a lot of practice, just like in any other language. However, this book provides you with key vocabulary, cultural phrases, and mental health terminology to assist your clients or future clients (if you are still undergoing training) throughout various stages of the counseling process.

Throughout the book the *¡Practique!* sections allow you to integrate and process what has been learned. I encourage you to complete these sections and repeat them as many times as possible in order to refine your skills. Also, throughout the chapters you will find *Cultural Hints* (denoted by this symbol [🫱]), segments that will allow you to integrate the language with the cultural nuances and the multicultural principles in order to avoid misunderstandings and to increase the chance of success in any cross-cultural and cross-linguistic interaction. Also, along with the book you will find the instructions to access the companion webiste that provides you with the correct pronunciations for all the sections of every chapter (those enclosed in a box with a [🔊 🎧] symbol). In order to remind ourselves that culture and people are so variable and that there are so many nuances within the Latino/Hispanic communities, the symbol [🚫] is used as a pictorial representation to avoid stereotyping. Just keep in mind that trends, common behaviors, and patterns are used to establish a base and foundation in an attempt to comprehend such a complex ethnic group. By using the companion website you will also have a chance to observe several case vignettes among Spanish-native speakers and non-native speakers. You will have the opportunity to integrate the writing, listening skills, and cultural nuances. Perhaps you are still a little bit skeptical about embarking on this linguistic journey. These are some common questions you have probably thought about already!:

Can I Learn Spanish or a Second Language at My Age?

Learning or refining a second language is not a task relegated only to children or adolescents. Although second language acquisition is certainly easier during childhood due to fewer social constrictions and minimal fear of failure, our brains are designed to acquire multiple languages (Cook, 1995; 1997). Since we counselors and psychologists are used to the academic rigor of college, learning a second language is just another learning activity. Perfectionism tends to be one of the biggest barriers that professionals encounter when learning a second language or mastering a new learning task (Cook, 2003). In fact, as you may already know, one of the favorite activities for retirees is learning a second language. One of the latest research studies about "brain-training" classes emphasizes the acquisition of a new language to keep the person's skills intact. The newest research comes from a large, well-designed study known as Advanced Cognitive Training for Independent and Vital Elderly (ACTIVE) (Willis, Tennstedt, Marsiske, Ball, Elias, Mann-Koepke, Morris, Rebok, Unversagt, Stoddard, & Wright, 2006). The study was conducted with 2,000 healthy seniors over a period of 5 years who received special training in specific mental functions (memory, reasoning, and speed of processing). Although learning new words and new languages are not the only ways of maintaining cognitive functions intact, the major finding about these types of related studies is that after short training regimens—10 sessions of 1 to 1.5 hours each over five or six weeks—improved mental functioning was kept as long as five years later. So if you are an active professional there is nothing that impedes you to learning the fundamentals of a new language. Age is not a valid excuse for not learning or refining a new language! Also, keep in mind that learning a second language promotes cultural sensitivity.

Why Should I Learn at Least Some Basic Spanish Skills?

The last Federal Census registered approximately 35 to 40 million Latinos/Hispanics living in the U.S.A. as a conservative figure (U.S. Bureau of the Census, 2000). The numbers are increasing and most states in the U.S.A. have seen a wave of Spanish-speaking clients. Being sensitive to the needs of Spanish-speaking clients is a sign of true multicultural embracement. Also, adding bilingual skills to your repertoire will certainly enhance your resume, curriculum vita, and job opportunities.

Is the Spanish Spoken in México the Same as That Spoken in El Salvador, Puerto Rico, Colombia, Cuba, Spain or Any of the Other Spanish-Speaking Countries? What Type of Spanish is Taught in This Book?

The communication among Spanish-native speakers from Latin America, the Spanish Caribbean (i.e., Puerto Rico, Dominican Republic, and Cuba), and Spain is as fluid as the communication among native English speakers from the U.S., Canada, New Zealand, England, Wales, Scotland, Ireland, and Australia. The accents vary as well as some cultural phrases and regionalisms that are the results of the hybridization of the language with indigenous and African words. However, the core of the Spanish language remains the same and intercommunication flows well among native speakers. On the other hand, to avoid misunderstandings and the use of words that may carry a different meaning or connotation among Spanish-speaking clients, *broadcast or generic Spanish* language is used throughout this book. Broadcast or generic Spanish is defined as a language free of cultural misinterpretations and it is typically used by Spanish-speaking professionals in Latin America and it is easily understood by all native speakers (Weller, 1983). As an illustration, this is the language used in Spanish soap operas filmed in Miami with a group of actors representing a myriad of countries from Latin America and Spain. The audience of these soap operas is from every part of the Latin American region.

What Is Different About This Book from Others in The Market?

This book is designed with the professional counselors and psychologists in mind and the situations that they run into on a daily basis. Most importantly, it is divided in sections by specialties or counseling branches (i.e., school counseling, mental health, and substance abuse) and embedded in a multicultural context. Other manuals or books in the market are designed for traveling and casual conversations and do not provide the counseling professional terminology and cultural background to address the needs of Spanish native speakers in a psychological or educational environment. Even those of us who are truly convinced of the intrinsic value of learning Spanish are compelled to come to terms with the practicality of such an endeavor. Is it practical? Yes! This book is written with the professional and school counselor, clinical and school psychologist, and social worker in mind who is not concerned with the technicalities of writing mechanics but with the common sense of a practitioner.

The book contains seven chapters that guide you from the cultural intricacies, history, and intra-diversity of Latinos/Hispanics to the counseling language and its application. The book gravitates towards two different directions; it provides linguistic information to you as a mental health provider and conversely offers cultural hints on how to work more effectively with Latino/Hispanic clients. The cultural aspect is critical to the understanding of the context and application of a word.

In sum, it is time to conquer your linguistic fears and commence a new stage in your professional development. I invite you to an exciting linguistic and cultural voyage that will enhance your counseling skills and open the window to a new world. *¡Bienvenidos y adelante!*

1   Who Are the Latinos/Hispanics?

A Brief Historical Overview of Their Culture and People

Latino/Hispanic Context in the United States (US)

As you might have already noticed, you can see and feel the presence of the Latino/Hispanic culture and the Spanish language everywhere in the US, from *rancheras* (Mexican native songs) in Virginia and Georgia, to *salsa* (Caribbean rhythm) in New York and Miami; Spanish radio stations in Chicago, New Mexico, and Texas; and *reggaeton* (a mix of reggae and salsa music) in Missouri, Orlando, and Los Angeles. Who has not enjoyed the delicious tacos, burritos, and *arroz con frijoles* (rice with beans) in restaurants throughout the nation? Who has not heard the captivating rhythms of Ricky Martin, Gloria Estefan, Marc Anthony, Jennifer López, Santana, Enrique Iglesias, Daddy Yankee, and Shakira? And who has not seen actors like Raúl Juliá, Andy García, Benicio del Toro, Penélope Cruz, and Javier Bardem on the big screen, in films made by the likes of Alejandro González Iñárritu (*Babel*), Pedro Almodóvar (*Volver*), Alfonso Cuarón (*Children of Men*), and Guillermo del Toro (*Pan's Labyrinth*)? What baseball fan has not heard of Sammy Sosa, Roberto Clemente, Alfonso Soriano, Roberto Alomar, Iván Rodríguez, Rod Carew, Fernando Valenzuela, Nomar Garciaparra, Alex Rodríguez, Alfonso Soriano, and Carlos Beltrán? And what about famous boxers such as Oscar de la Hoya, Tito Trinidad, Julio César Chávez, Roberto Durán, Héctor "Macho" Camacho, and Miguel Cotto? The Latino/Hispanic culture is gradually increasing its presence in our lives, and as a result, influencing and enriching our US culture. Its contributions have spiced up the US and added an exquisite flavor to the already eclectic and diverse US culture.

There are over 900 Spanish publications in the US, from magazines for teenagers, men, and women to major newspapers (Allied Media Hispanic Publication Network, 2009). The presence of Spanish soap operas on TV and major TV channels such as Telemundo, MTV Latino, and CNN in Spanish are markets that have more than 5 million viewers in the US (Allied Media Hispanic Publication Network, 2009). An article from the Mediamark Reporter database (2010) showed that approximately 7,719,000 Latinos/Hispanics watch the popular Spanish cable network, Galavisión, while over 38 million Latinos/Hispanics watch MTV (Fall

2010 Demographics – Household: Spanish or Hispanic Origin or Descent, 2010). English as a second language (ESL), English Language Learner (ELL), and Bilingual programs (BP) are flourishing nationwide in school districts, colleges, and community colleges. The most popular non-English language in high schools and colleges is Spanish, ahead of French, German, Japanese, Mandarin, and Arabic. It is very likely that you have noticed a myriad of job advertisements on electronic media and in traditional newspapers announcing: "*Bilingual skills with conversational knowledge of Spanish preferred.*" Today, we are living in a nation that it is becoming increasingly bilingual, much like Canada with its Francophone population.

Although there is considerable poverty among Latinos/Hispanics, just like in any other ethnic group represented in the US, not all Latinos/Hispanics are underprivileged or lacking in acquisition power. The Latino/Hispanic consumer market is close to US $500 billion a year (CUNY Graduate Center, 2009). Latinos/Hispanics are spending more on food, cleaning and laundry supplies, and personal and household items (Felsch, 2006). In addition, Latino/Hispanic families spend an average of $133 on groceries each week, while the average US household spends $92.50 (Felsch, 2006). Latinos/Hispanics are people who believe in the "American dream" of having a job and owning a home; in fact, 48.9 percent of Latinos/Hispanics are homeowners (Kochlar, Gonzalez-Barrera & Dockerman, 2009). Therefore, Latinos/Hispanics are injecting their money into the US economy instead of depending on government assistance, which is a popularmis conception. In fact, mindful of the Latino/Hispanic market's potential, academic institutions such as DePaul University in Chicago and Florida State University are offering a "Hispanic Marketing" specialty with the sole intent of tailoring specific strategies to target the Latino/Hispanic population in the US (Cohen, 2007). In the same vein, advertisement companies are investing millions of dollars in order to reach this growing sector of the US population. It is interesting to know that according to *Forbes* magazine the richest man in the world is a Mexican citizen, Carlos Slim Helú (Forbes, 2010). He is the chairman and chief executive of the telecommunications companies Telmex and América Móvil and has extensive holdings in other Mexican companies through his conglomerate, Grupo Carso S.A.B., as well as business interests elsewhere in the world.

Because of these statistical figures and in recognition of the massive force and power of this ethnic group, politicians are tailoring their campaigns to Latinos/Hispanics nationwide but especially in New York, Miami, Orlando, L.A., Texas, and New Mexico, where the Latino/Hispanic vote could decisively change the course of any electoral outcome. It is not uncommon these days to hear political candidates inserting Spanish phrases into their political campaigns in order to catch the attention of this segment of the population. In sum, Latinos/Hispanics are here to stay and cannot be ignored by educational, political, and economic sectors. Most importantly, they cannot be ignored by mental health professionals!

Who Are the Latino/Hispanic People?

Since the unfiltered mass media is not always the most reliable vehicle for obtaining information about the complexities and uniqueness of ethnic groups, it is of utmost importance to demystify the origin of the Latino/Hispanic people in the US For those who have limited experience traveling outside the boundaries of the US and have lived only in a particular part of the country, it is easy to associate the phrase "Latino/Hispanic" with a specific ethnic group such as Mexican, Puerto Rican, or Cuban, because these may be the largest national ethnicities represented within a particular Latino/Hispanic community (Lopez & Dockterman, 2011). However, remember that there are 20 Spanish-speaking countries in Latin America and two in Europe: Spain and Andorra, which is French/Spanish bilingual; also, Belize's official language is English, but Spanish is widely spoken as well. These countries are all represented in the Latino/Hispanic community in the US (Ortiz-Cotto, 2011), and have been for centuries. The idea that Latinos/Hispanics are newcomers to the US is not true: keep in mind that there are Latino/Hispanic people whose ancestors inhabited the south-west and west (e.g. Texas, California, New Mexico, Arizona) of North America even before the formation of the US as a nation. It is, however, correct to say that there has been an explosive demographic growth in the last 50 years as a result of immigration and natural increases (births minus deaths).

What Does History Mean to the Current Latinos/Hispanics in the US and Latin America?

It is of utmost importance to be aware of the historical, political, colonial, and racial background of our Latino/Hispanic neighbors to the south because these are the people who are immigrating to the US and are potential clients that you will be working with in schools and agencies. These are people who have a rich history and come from different economic, educational, and racial sectors of Latin American society. Being appreciative of clients' backgrounds and history will help us to place their linguistic and cultural needs in a historical framework and social context. As counselors, psychologists, and social workers, it is easy to dismiss our clients' culture as an abbreviated textbook definition or a set of dos and don'ts, without reflecting on their complex histories.

For instance, several years ago when I was working for a community agency in Oregon, I had a court-ordered case relating to child abuse. The case had been reassigned to me because the parents were immigrants from Mexico and unable to speak English. Even though I am a native Spanish speaker and Latino/Hispanic, I went to the first family visit with the preconceived idea that these clients would be similar to many of the traditional Mexican clients that I had seen in the past (although, of course, there is no such thing as traditional or typical in any culture). To my surprise, as I interacted with them for the first time, I noticed a different intonation and accent that deviated from any Mexican pronunciation from the south, north or center of the country that I was used to hearing. I also noticed that the parents had difficulties articulating and organizing their thoughts as I conducted the intake interview.

Since both parents had exactly the same difficulties with the language, I ruled out cognitive deficiency or a specific mental health diagnosis. After I made inquiries regarding the region in Mexico that they had immigrated from, I learned that Spanish was their second language and Tarascan (*Tarasco* or *Purepecha*, a native indigenous language) was their mother tongue! Furthermore, these clients did not even consider themselves Latinos/Hispanics, but Tarascan indigenous people coming from the area of Michoacán in Mexico; this was their primary national and ethnic identity. Working with these clients taught me a lesson about the overgeneralization and simplification of cultures and how critical is to have a more in-depth understanding of Latino/Hispanic immigrants in the US

Racial and Ethnic Diversity among Latinos/Hispanics

If somebody were to ask you to describe what a typical Latino/Hispanic looks like, what would you say? Your response should be "There is no typical Latino/Hispanic!" Yes, it is possible that you may find a significant number of individuals in certain countries who resemble the stereotypical image of a Latino/Hispanic as portrayed by the media (e.g. short stature, dark skin, brown eyes, and black hair), but this would be a risky generalization. Latinos/Hispanics are called the rainbow people because you may find all skin colors represented and all sorts of beautiful ethnic combinations! That being said, racism and discrimination, like in the US or any other nation in the world, also persists in Latin America in covert or overt ways depending on the country and its history.

The Critical Mistake: All Latinos/Hispanics Under One Umbrella

From the beginning of the influx of Latinos/Hispanics in the US since the end of the nineteenth century, there has been an evolution of ethnic labels to categorize them. For instance, in the nineteenth century, the umbrella term *Hispano* was first used on the West Coast by those who were of Spanish descent coming from Mexico to populate North America. This term separated *Hispanos* from those who did not have a Spanish lineage. However, on the East Coast, the term *Spanish* was used to differentiate those of European background from those of mixed heritage (e.g., Black, Indian, Asian, Muslim, or Jewish). This characterization gave the man advantage in the northern Anglo-dominated culture, which preferred Europeans over other nationalities.

From the early 1900s until the 1940s, the term *Latin* was coined in many circles to identify those whose main language was either Spanish or any other Romance language (e.g., Italian, Portuguese, French). The term was not closely associated with a specific country of origin but mostly with physical and personal traits such as being dark, attractive, mysterious, and romantic: the image of the legendary Latin lover, as portrayed by the media and Hollywood movies (Novas, 2008).

In the 1940s and 1950s, the US Census instituted a new category to classify those who came from Latin America or Spain or whose primary language was Spanish; this category was the *Spanish surname*. This category was not an efficient one; in fact, the government produced a list of over 600 Spanish surnames (e.g. López, Castro, Martínez) but in the process omitted those Latinos/Hispanics who did not have a Spanish surname. Furthermore, this new categorization prompted some Latinos/Hispanics to change their surnames to avoid discrimination and marginalization, just as German immigrants did after World War II. Naturally, this form of classification did not ameliorate the confusion relating to Latinos/Hispanics.

To "simplify" matters and for categorical purposes," the US Federal Census Bureau created the *Hispanic* racial category in the 1970s (Benitez, 2007). Individuals whose primary racial identification was Hispanic had to meet at least one of the following two criteria:

(a) the primary language spoken at home was Spanish, or
(b) either they or their ancestors were immigrants of a Latin American country or Spain.

The situation became complicated for the US Federal Census Bureau, hospitals, schools, and social service agencies, when new immigrants were puzzled by this categorization process in which they had to identify themselves with a racial category that did not accurately reflect their ethnic background. In fact, until a decade ago, the Hispanic ethnic label was believed to be a distinct race by many state and federal agencies.

National and state statistical figures were confused all the more when it was realized that many Latinos/Hispanics identified themselves as white (Caucasian), black (African descent), Indian or Native Indian, Asian, or other categories. Others, prior to coming to the US, did not see themselves as belonging to a particular "racial" category due to the high level of ethnic mix (*mestizaje*) in their countries of origin. As a consequence, instead of having a racial identity, as encouraged in the US, many Latin Americans embraced a national identity (e.g. Mexican (*mejicano*), Salvadorian (*salvadoreño*), or Peruvian (*peruano*), which distinguished them from other Latinos/Hispanics. Acknowledging the complexity of the situation, the federal government updated its primary ethnic categorizations to reflect more accurately the background of Latinos/Hispanics. As a result, the following categorization of Latinos/Hispanics was used in the 2010 US Census questionnaire (see Sample Items No. 5 and No. 6 below):

---

5. Is this person of Hispanic, Latino, or Spanish origin?

☐ No, not of Hispanic, Latino, or Spanish origin
☐ Yes, Mexican, Mexican Am., Chicano
☐ Yes, Puerto Rican
☐ Yes, Cuban
☐ Yes, another Hispanic, Latino, or Spanish origin – *Print origin, for example, Argentinean, Colombian, Dominican, Nicaraguan, Salvadoran, Spaniard, and so on.*

Race.

---

6. What is this person's race? *Mark ☑ one or more boxes.*

☐ White
☐ Black, African Am., or Negro
☐ American Indian or Alaska Native – *Print name of enrolled or principal tribe.*

☐ Asian Indian   ☐ Chinese   ☐ Native Hawaiian
☐ Chinese   ☐ Korean   ☐ Guamanian or Chamorro
☐ Filipino   ☐ Vietnamese   ☐ Samoan

☐ Other Asian – *Print race, for example, Hmong, Laotian, Thai, Pakistani, Cambodian and so on.*   ☐ Other Pacific Islander – *Print race, for example, Fijian, Tongan, and so on.*

☐ Some other race – *Print race.*

Latino/Hispanic Identity

Since 1970 the US Census questionnaire has asked US residents whether they are of Hispanic origin, and if so, which broad Hispanic group they identify with. Hispanic origin is considered separately from race in the Census—and Hispanics may identify with any race. As the largest and fastest-growing ethnic minority in the United States, the information about Hispanic origin is of growing importance. It is used in numerous programs and for monitoring equal employment opportunities.

The 2010 questionnaire lists 15 racial categories, and includes space to write specific races not listed on the form. The 2010 Census also contains the option first introduced in the 2000 Census for respondents to choose more than one race. Only about 2 percent of Americans identified with more than one race in the 2000 Census, but the percentage was much higher for children and young adults, and this will likely increase.

Hispanic or Latino?

Using the correct terminology when referring to a client who belongs to an underrepresented ethnic group can be challenging for all of us as we try to be sensitive to their background. However, it is especially challenging for mental health professionals who want to be in tune with the needs of their clients, rather than merely wanting to satisfy politically correct policies. Many Latin Americans dislike the term *Hispanic* because they are not of Spanish-European extraction. Since they do not have a connection with Spain, they would rather use the romance language roots and culture to accentuate their background; consequently, the term *Latino* (masculine) or *Latina* (feminine) has been embraced by many people in the US who have felt ethnically disenfranchised and have found a source of unity and commonality. Also, for many, using the word *Latino* has been an opportunity to redefine their ethnic identity according to their own history and reality.

However, for recent immigrants coming from Latin America, the country of origin seems to be more important than a generic term (i.e. *Latino* or *Hispanic*), which doesn't necessarily encompass the complexity of their national past (i.e. Ecuadorian, Bolivian, Chilean, and Uruguayan). However, since not all Latinos/Hispanics think alike, and since we are aware of their intricate history, the best option for mental health professionals is to ask our clients their country of origin (or that of their ancestors) and their preferred ethnic identification. In sum, it is essential that you do not make any stereotypical assumptions relative to your Latino/Hispanic clients when it comes to ethnicity or racial identification. Always ask!

Since All of You Are Latinos/Hispanics, You Should Get Along with Each Other

Just as between many other neighboring nations in the world, there are many existing tensions between Latin Americans, and these are mainly rooted in territorial disputes (sometimes involving war), sport (e.g. soccer, boxing, and basketball), cultural superiority, and racial discrimination; the advancement of economic power and educational achievement has also fomented class divisions and strains that are sometimes associated with their countries of origin. It is clear to all nations in the world that people will not necessarily get along with each other just because they live geographically close, look alike, speak the same language, and engage in similar cultural and religious activities. Like any other human beings, Latinos/Hispanics may also hold biases and prejudices against their fellow Latinos/Hispanics. Therefore, the concept of homogeneity among Latinos/Hispanics is a myth.

Homogeneity is a fallacy that does not apply to any ethnic or racial group. Nonetheless, there are certain elements that unify people from certain cultures. In this case, Latinos/Hispanics share a series of elements that in some ways unites them. When they leave their countries of origin and establish residency in a culturally and linguistically different environment such as the US or Europe, they are forced to look at their similarities, and minimize their differences, therefore creating a process of unification among individuals of Latino/Hispanic heritage.

Most Latinos/Hispanics can understand the realities of their Latin American neighbors. Marked exceptions apply to ethnic indigenous groups, which remain somewhat isolated from mainstream societies in Latin America.

Linguistic Diversity

Spanish is the dominant language in Latin America as a result of a colonization process that took hundreds of years. Nevertheless, there are many Latin Americans whose first language is a native indigenous language. According to Campbell (1997), there are approximately 550–700 native indigenous languages and dialects spoken in Latin America. Although Spanish is the official language of most Latin American countries (with the exception of Brazil, Belize, and Jamaica), many sectors of their populations continue using their native languages as their primary form of communication. The prevalence of non-Spanish languages typically depends on the native indigenous population sizes. For instance, countries like Bolivia, Peru, and Guatemala have large numbers of indigenous inhabitants who keep their cultures and traditions alive by using their native languages. Then again, in more homogeneous populations like Puerto Rico, the Dominican Republic, or Cuba, where no one speaks the original native languages, Spanish is the lingua franca. Similarly, Argentina, Uruguay, and Paraguay have very low numbers of native indigenous people, and so the Spanish language prevails. Code switching (switching from Spanish to another language and vice versa) in many Latin American countries is a very common practice. Likewise, countries in which the people are close to the Brazilian border tend to be proficient in Portuguese due to their proximity and for business reasons.

Cultural hints: Out of politeness and to avoid any type of conflict, if asked, most Latinos/Hispanics would deny the existence of cultural/ethnic preference, discrimination, or racism in their country of origin.

Cultural hints: The origin of the word *mulato* comes from the Spanish word *mula* (mule). That is, the sterile offspring of a donkey and a horse. Although the word is accepted in many circles, it is distasteful, outdated, and based on the slavery conceptualization of the Spanish conquistadors. The terms *biracial* or *multiethnic* are more suitable and consistent with multicultural literature.

Cultural hints: *Criollos* are considered to be the direct descendants of Spanish ancestors, who were born in Latin America but can trace their roots back to the old continent.

Natural Demographic Growth (Birth) of Latinos/Hispanics Versus Immigration Patterns

The following series of graphs provide a detailed picture of Latinos/Hispanics in the US These offer information about population demographics, intermarriages, levels of education, income earnings, and occupational distributions.

The Operationalization of Multicultural Counseling Competencies as Emphasized by the American Counseling Association (ACA)

One of the key aspects of multicultural competencies is the operationalization of its counseling competencies (Sue, Arredondo & MacDavis, 1992). Traditionally, the challenge has been to put diversity principles into practice in such a way that the clients can benefit. The following are three exemplary elements that allow practitioners to gauge whether or not we are in the process of achieving multicultural competency.

U.S. Hispanic Population

BY COUNTRY OF ORIGIN, 2010

Mexican	31,798,000
Puerto Rican	4,624,000
Cuban	1,786,000
Salvadoran	1,649,000
Dominican	1,415,000
Guatemalan	1,044,000
Colombian	909,000
Honduran	633,000
Ecuadorian	565,000
Peruvian	531,000

Figure 1.1 U.S. Latino/Hispanic population

Source: Pew Research Center 2011

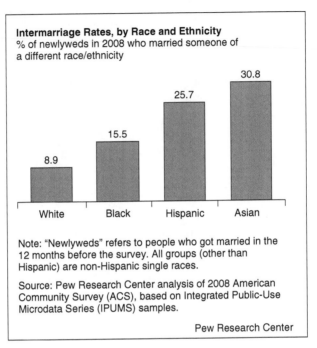

Figure 1.2 Intermarriages among Latinos/Hispanics, Whites, Blacks, and Asians

Knowledge-Base and Understanding of Background

Understanding the complex history of Latinos/Hispanics in the US is the first step to comprehending that many of them are not newcomers to this country, but have been among the first inhabitants of certain regions of the country since the foundation of the USA nunderstanding of their worldviews and history of oppression allows the counselor to see that this is an extremely eclectic ethnic group.

Table 1.1 Level of education (educational attainment)

	At least high school graduate		College graduate or more	
	Men	*Women*	*Men*	*Women*
White, non-Hispanic	89.9	90.1	32.9	28.4
Black	80.4	80.8	16.6	18.5
Hispanic	57.3	59.5	11.8	12.3

Note: Age 25 and over shown, available at: www.census.gov/populations/socdemo/education/cps2004/tab01a-01.pdf

Source: US Census Bureau (2005). Tables 1a, 01, –03, –04, and –06

Table 1.2 Household income[a] distribution by race and ethnicity, 1973–2003

Year	Non-Hispanic White					Non-Hispanic Black					Hispanic Percent Distribution				
	Under $14,999	$15,000–$49,999	$50,000–$99,999	$100,000 or More	Median Household Income (Dollars)	Under $14,999	$15,000–$49,999	$50,000–$99,999	$100,000 or More	Median Household Income (Dollars)	Under $14,999	$15,000–$49,999	$50,000–$99,999	$100,000 or More	Median Household Income (Dollars)
1973	17.0	45.9	30.8	6.3	$39,859	34.0	49.3	15.2	1.5	$23,257	21.7	57.6	19.0	1.7	$29,207
1975	17.7	48.7	28.6	5.0	$37,467	36.4	48.6	14.0	1.0	$22,324	25.6	57.3	15.5	1.6	$26,715
1980	16.4	45.8	30.7	7.1	$40,206	35.8	46.5	16.0	1.7	$22,760	24.1	52.7	20.4	2.8	$28,864
1985	15.6	44.3	30.8	9.3	$41,527	34.1	46.0	17.3	2.6	$24,163	26.3	50.3	20.1	3.3	$30,475
1990	14.1	43.1	31.3	11.5	$43,597	33.7	43.6	18.6	4.1	$25,488	24.3	50.0	21.0	4.7	$30,475
1995	13.8	41.8	31.4	13.0	$44,564	30.5	45.2	20.2	4.1	$26,842	26.8	49.7	18.9	4.6	$27,401
2000	13.0	38.3	31.6	17.1	$48,734	24.7	45.6	22.7	7.0	$31,690	17.9	49.2	25.7	7.2	$35,429
2003	13.4	38.3	31.0	17.3	$47,777	27.4	44.3	21.6	6.7	$29,645	18.9	50.1	23.5	7.5	$32,997

[a] In 2003 Dollars

Source: DeNavas–Walt et al. 2004

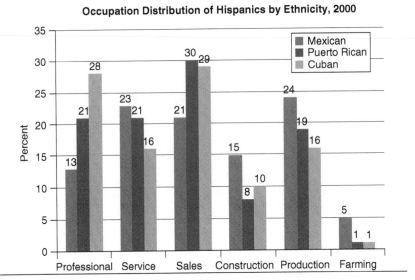

Figure 1.3 Occupational distribution

Source: Pew Research Center, 2005

Eradication of Ethnic Myths

Myths and misconceptions abound about Latinos/Hispanics in the US Most of these myths are based on preconceived notions or on a lack of solid evidence relative to their reality. Unfortunately, the media and biased newspaper or magazine articles have played a role in the creation of myths relative to immigration, job losses, crime, education, religion, family, and alcohol use, among other things. One of the first steps to becoming a more transparent professional is to remove the myths that taint our therapeutic filters.

Developing Sensitivity and Empathy

Once we have understood their historical, social, ethnic, racial, religious, and family background, we are then able to demystify some of the preconceived notions that impede our ability to reach a level of empathy and sensitivity towards our Latino/Hispanic clients. Unlike other therapeutic constructs, empathy and sensitivity cannot be "taught," only encouraged.

2 Cultural Norms and Family Systems

Considerations in the Latino/Hispanic Culture

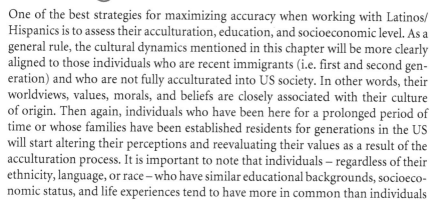 As has been repeated throughout the book, attempting to identify so-called "universal" variables among any ethnic group is likely to be an exercise infutility because of the vast intra-ethnic and individual differences involved; and of course, we run the risk of stereotyping people, which is precisely what this book sets out to discourage. In fact, after looking at general descriptors of an ethnic group, one could easily say, "Well, that does not sound or look like me." Although this is true, we have to keep in mind that some aspects are more prevalent (to a greater or lesser extent) among certain ethnic groups, and this is also the case with Latinos/ Hispanics. The purpose of this section is therefore to provide a cultural platform from which non-Latino/Hispanic mental health professionals can observe general dynamics and have a better conceptualization of this group of people. Nothing here replaces the clinical judgment of a social worker or psychologist, or of a school, mental health, or substance abuse counselor. But it is hoped that eventually you will formulate the conclusions of your evaluations based on a combination of several assessment tools, one of which will be a sound consideration of cultural elements.

Acculturation

One of the best strategies for maximizing accuracy when working with Latinos/ Hispanics is to assess their acculturation, education, and socioeconomic level. As a general rule, the cultural dynamics mentioned in this chapter will be more clearly aligned to those individuals who are recent immigrants (i.e. first and second generation) and who are not fully acculturated into US society. In other words, their worldviews, values, morals, and beliefs are closely associated with their culture of origin. Then again, individuals who have been here for a prolonged period of time or whose families have been established residents for generations in the US will start altering their perceptions and reevaluating their values as a result of the acculturation process. It is important to note that individuals – regardless of their ethnicity, language, or race – who have similar educational backgrounds, socioeconomic status, and life experiences tend to have more in common than individuals who share the same ethnicity or nationality but have different levels of education and socioeconomic experiences. Furthermore, children and adolescents tend to acculturate and adapt at faster rates than adults. They tend to be more malleable and flexible than their adult counterparts because they have "less cultural baggage" to negotiate, such as memories, cultural norms, and linguistic standards. Consequently, the cultural assessment process must be conducted differently according to these distinctively different age groups. More information on assessment tests and inventories will be provided in Chapters 4, 5, and 6 with respect to client age groups (i.e. children, adolescents, adults) and specialized disciplines (i.e. school counseling, mental health, substance abuse, psychology).

La familia (*Family*)

The family is the primary unit and the center of support among Latinos/Hispanics and has a strong cultural foundation (Nuño, Dorrington & Alvarez, 1998). Historically, during times of oppression and abuse, Latin American citizens (regardless of their country of origin) have always sought shelter, protection, and support within the family unit. Since colonial times, family members learned to keep secrets and guard their own from oppressors. So the centuries-old met a message is that no one cares more than the family, and support (i.e. economic, political, legal, and social) must be provided for the family in all circumstances and conditions. There is a saying in Latino/Hispanic culture that exemplifies this statement: "*la sangre pesa más que el agua*" (literally, "blood is heavier than water"), similar to the English saying, "blood is thicker than water." The family is seen as the core for functionality and progress, and all relevant decisions are made within its circle; this is based on the principles of centeredness and collectivism. This pride in the extended family, expressed through the maintenance of close ties and strong obligations to kinfolk, is defined as *familismo* (familism). Typically, personal issues are kept within the family, as this Latino/Hispanicsaying exemplifies: "*los paños sucios se lavan en casa*" (literally, "dirty rags are washed at home"), similar to the English saying, "don't wash your dirty linen in public."

A good starting place for any discussion of Latino/Hispanic culture is therefore with *la familia* (the family). Family involvement often is critical for the health care of your clients. Traditionally, Latinos/Hispanics include many people as part of their extended families: not only parents and siblings, but grandparents, aunts, uncles, cousins, close friends, and godparents (*padrinos*) of the family's children. When ill or injured, Latino/Hispanic people frequently consult with other family members and often ask them to come along to medical visits. Latino/Hispanic extended families and the support role they play for clients may run counter to certain institutional rules, such as hospital policies that limit patients to two visitors. You may encounter similar situations when one of your clients may solicit permission to have a family member participate or be present at a counseling session. This request may initially catch you off guard and you will have to negotiate with tact the concept of individual counseling. For instance, a good strategy can be to have the other person (i.e. cousin, aunt, or other person selected by your client) present partially during the first session as you explain the importance of individuation and personal growth to both of them and how this will benefit the entire family in the long run. If the concept of individual counseling is presented in terms of the end result benefiting the whole family unit, this will typically this be received with open arms.

Machismo

There are certain stereotypical customs in all cultures and ethnic groups that are taken as their trademark, be they positive or negative. From these, we develop traces of prejudice or favoritism against or in favor of certain groups. For example, when *machismo* is mentioned in reference to Latino/Hispanic men, an array of traits is automatically associated with it: the exercise of psychological and physical control, patriarchy, abuse, consumption of large amounts of alcohol, and womanizing. Machismo in this negative sense is based on the myth that men are superior to women, intellectually, physically, and psychologically. This *negative machismo* is based on two very disparate descriptions of men and women. In this view, women are seen as being docile, fragile, sentimental, dependent, faithful, emotionally weak, seductive, and in need of protection. In contrast, men are viewed as being strong, imaginative, assertive, independent, intellectually profound, providers, and emotionally strong (Mirandé, 1997). The concept of *negative machismo* entails privileges and authoritarian rule for men. Unfortunately, this worldview leads to problems in health care and legal issues. For instance, men who hold the belief that they can have multiple romantic affairs (while women cannot) because they are macho and have the "right" may also believe that there is no need to practice safe sex, as they are too strong and healthy to get any disease. This can lead to HIV infections and sexually transmitted diseases that can affect the health of their spouses (Zombrana, 1995). Likewise, the exaggerated consumption of alcohol to prove masculinity and physical strength leads to confrontations with the law (Padilla, 1995). This worldview of control and power has its roots in the colonial history of the Spanish conquest in which the *conquistadores* came to dominate the land, resources, and the native indigenous people by force. Male superiority was a precept to promote the conquest of the savage world in the Americas (Limón, 1998).

However, there is another side of machismo that has been portrayed as *romantic machismo*. This view describes the man as gentle, caring, responsible, a hard worker, family-oriented, and in love with only one woman. This type of machismo has been presented in literature and offers the notion of a sensitive man who respects women and sees them as equals (Abalos, 2002; Moraga, 1993). Unfortunately, the narrative that is stuck in the collective psyche of our society is the negative and abusive one, whereby these views and practices are being encouraged not only by some men in Latino/Hispanic society, but also by those in other societies as well. There are also many women who themselves embrace machismo and are victims of this dysfunctional paradigm that has been ingrained by centuries of gender oppression (as detailed in the following section).

Hembrismo

Hembrismo is the counterpart to *machismo*, and describes the role of the female specifically in the presence of *machismo*. There is an interaction at work that accentuates these two concepts. *Hembrismo* is the view that women have moral and spiritual superiority over men. According to this definition, women are motivated by honor and reputation, and should therefore be submissive and patient with their husbands (Nida, 1974). For instance, when their husbands engage in extramarital affairs, this moral superiority is demonstrated when the wives ignore the moral failure of their husbands and take some of the responsibility themselves. They should ask themselves: "Am I attractive enough to keep my husband with me?" and "What have I done that has made him want to search for other women?" They should tell themselves: "It is my responsibility to keep my family intact, so I will ignore what he does outside the home."

The role of mothers in Latin American cultures has spiritual qualities and connotations, which brings stability to homes and society in general. This view has strong religious overtones based on a widespread devotion to the Virgin Mary. In fact, even the visual arts portray Mary as caring, close, and radiant in spite of the suffering around her, while Jesus and God are presented as stern, powerful, and distant. Therefore, *hembrismo* is rooted in *Marianismo*, which is the cult of the Virgin Mary and the exaltation of all her attributes and qualities, which should be imitated by women. Devotion to husbands, children, and family should take precedence over personal needs (Bueno & Ceasar, 1998). That being said, this phenomenon is less observed in educated professional women who have pursued a career and have been exposed to diverse lifestyles. This is also less pertinent for women who are less religious or have less association with Catholic practices.

Patriarcalismo (*Patriarchalism*)

A patriarchal system is a form of social organization in which the man is the head of the family and the family name is traced through the male line (Mayo, 1997). Throughout human history, most societies have been patriarchal in nature and male dominated. However, through the advent of human rights, education, and equality, many patriarchal systems in most Western-industrialized societies have experienced remarkable changes, bringing gender equality to the forefront. In many ways, *patriarcalismo* (patriarchalism) is seen as an extension of *machismo* and is based on the idea of male supremacy. This phenomenon is reflected in the family, the workplace, education, politics, and society at large. In many Latino/ Hispanic families, the decision-making process is led by the father, and the final decisions are made by him because, as the breadwinner and head of the household, he feels entitled to do so. There is also a belief that having firm control of the family equates to being a man (which is linked to *machismo*) (Mayo, 1997). *Patriarcalismo* also signifies that a man will have a preference for having a boy over a girl because a boy will preserve the family name, and, in a subtle way, this will demonstrate the virility of the father by having another male. (⊗) Again, beware of stereotyping! This is not necessarily true in many well-educated, open-minded, and cosmopolitan Latino/Hispanic families in which equality between the parents is essential, dialogue among family members is at the forefront of family relationships, and there is no justification for one member to make decisions for the rest (Sotomayor, 1991).

Mind, Body, and Spirit

Health care and mental health professionals often work within the structures of mainstream medicine, which provides separate physical and mental health care. Training programs emphasize the thoughts (cognition), feelings (emotions), and actions (behavior) of clients' understanding that these dimensions can either be observed or measured; therefore, a positivist/medical model is typically used as a guide for treatment. Although spirituality is mentioned more frequently in the literature and at professional conventions, there is still hesitancy regarding the best way to deal with this aspect. The reality is that not all mental health professionals are devoutly religious individuals, and since many mental health agencies and schools have strict policies related to religious indoctrination, mental health professionals opt to either minimize or circumvent spiritual themes of conversation (Corey, Callanan & Schneider-Corey, 2010). (⊗) On the other hand, the general Latino/Hispanic worldview is firmly rooted in the idea of a higher power that often intervenes in their daily lives. Consequently, Latinos/Hispanics tend to view health from a more synergistic point of view. This view is expressed as the continuum of mind, body, and spirit (*espíritu*). For instance, the concepts of *mal de ojo* (the evil eye), *brujería* (witchcraft), *espiritismo* (spiritism), and *santería* (supernatural magic) are manifestations and expressions of the myriad of beliefs that have resulted from the merging of Catholicism with indigenous and African religions in the Americas (Mullner & Giachello, 2011). Some clients may attribute some of their mental and medical health issues or disturbances to the influence of spiritual forces. It is not advisable to ignore the importance of the spirit (*espíritu*) and how it affects health in general. While there is no need to get into profound theological or hermeneutic dialogues, mental health professionals must not avoid this topic of conversation if it is brought to their attention; rather, it should be addressed with respect and should be connected to their current issues. The utilization of a third party (e.g. a priest, reverend, or healer) at some point during the therapy process should not be discarded as a possible intervention strategy.

Formalities and Etiquette Generalities

Broadly speaking, Latinos/Hispanics have a tendency for formality among themselves, especially when they do not know each other well. As a greeting or to say goodbye, a firm hand-shake, a hug, or a kiss on one cheek are common between women, and between women and men, and in some South American countries and Spain, between men as well. The Spanish language provides different forms of speech for formal and informal address (in the use of both *usted* and *tú* for the pronoun *you*, formal and familiar forms of commands, and the use of titles of respect before people's first names such as *Don* or *Doña*). Since there is no *usted* in English, and there is only "you" for both formal and informal use, non-Spanish speakers may seem to be too informal or irreverent toward adults. Likewise, the use of professional, political, or religious titles is seriously observed. For example, "Doctor Rodríguez" (Dr. Rodríguez), "Licenciado Martínez" (Attorney Martínez), "Sacerdote Ruíz" (Priest/Father Ruíz), "Ingeniero Rosas" (Engineer Rosas), and "Profesor Pérez" (Professor Pérez). In contrast, during informal conversations among friends and family, the pace is fast, somewhat loud, and accompanied by animated gestures and body language to accentuate a point (Gessler, 1991). In fact, from afar and for a non-native Spanish speaker, these conversations can give the impression of being a shouting match.

Now that you have familiarized yourself with Latino/Hispanic history in the U.S. and have a notion of the ethnic, racial, national, and social complexity of this group, along with its unique family and systemic elements, you are ready to tackle an introduction and review of the Spanish language. First of all, relax and have fun! Put on your linguistic hat, set aside the overly analytical and detail-oriented part of our professions, and try to bring alive the moments when you learned some basic Spanish skills in high school or college. Before going over the alphabet and basic language skills, make a list of all the frustrations, fears, or concerns that you have with regard to embarking on this linguistic journey. It is easy to over-rationalize every pronunciation, enunciation, accent, or grammar rule and in the process get stuck in the details. To avoid a microscopic approach, I encourage you to look at the bigger picture. Comprehension, understanding, and basic communication are the key aspects of this process. Make reference to the *reader's companion website* at any time, and above all, practice, practice, and practice. Learning the basics of a second language should come naturally and should not be a painful task; instead, it should be a pleasant cognitive and cultural journey. Enjoy, and *¡buena suerte!* (good luck!)

3   An Introduction to and Review of the Spanish Language

Language Acquisition Tips

Typically when I am conducting language training workshops at schools, hospitals, or mental health agencies, I have been asked the following questions:

(a)   How can I learn Spanish quickly?
(b)   What are the best strategies for not forgetting what I have learned?
(c)   How long does it take to be completely fluent in Spanish?
(d)   Does my accent impede communication with some clients?
(e)   Why am I having difficulty retaining some concepts?

The answers to all these questions will vary depending on a lot of factors, not all of which can be fully predicted or explained. As mentioned in the preface of this book, many of us have to combat many preconceived ideas and met a messages that have been culturally and educationally ingrained through the years. For instance, during an in-service workshop at a school district, I had a fellow school counselor who jotted down and shared the following thoughts with the group: "I feel awkward," "I feel dumb and slow," "I don't like to be the last one in class," "I feel incompetent," "I cannot learn at my age," and so on. These are not atypical irrational and negative messages; on the contrary, this list is fairly common. Unfortunately, these are negative messages that we have learned and internalized for a long time and that are impeding our acquisition of a second language. The following is a list of tips and recommendations that may help you to acquire, understand, and process the Spanish language in a more fluid, logical, and natural way:

(1)   As you attempt to learn and memorize, begin with an empty slate. That is, using a basic cognitive behavioral technique, identify what are and have been the irrational thoughts that have hampered your ability to learn a new language fluently in the past. Jot down the thoughts that come to mind and create a list. Your job as a student of culture and language is to cognitively and emotionally fight back and combat these messages and allow your brain to absorb the new information without cognitive blockages.

(2) Designate a place and time at home that facilitates your Spanish learning process. Devote between 25 minutes and an hour daily to reading, writing, and listening in Spanish.

(3) Use your time effectively. Turn off the TV, watch fewer useless programs and motivate yourself to get into a productive and useful routine of learning.

(4) Find out the time of the day when you are most receptive to learning. Once the best time is identified, stick to the routine. With time, this should become second nature.

(5) Use the time in your car and turn on the Spanish radio station. You will be amazed how all of the sudden you will start picking up words, concepts, and even full sentences. Most importantly, pay attention to slang and commonly used phrases.

(6) Rent movies in Spanish, especially Latin American (South and Central American) films, instead of the ones filmed in Spain. The Castilian accent is a little bit harder to follow, just as British or Irish accents are for Americans.

7) Think in Spanish. Attempt to say or identify day-to-day objects, events, and places, and create sentences in Spanish. Have internal conversations in Spanish even when you are not devoting your time to your formal studies.

(8) If you normally go to the gym, walk or run, record your voice and play it back during your exercise sessions. Memorization will occur naturally.

(9) Devote time to meet a native speaker at a school, community college, church, or in your community. Some community colleges sponsor partnership programs, and these can be a great opportunity to start a cultural relationship and potential friendship.

(10) Volunteer time at a community center that provides services to Spanish-speaking populations. Being surrounded by native Spanish speakers will allow you to absorb the culture and language simultaneously.

(11) Use your lunch hour efficiently and practice your vocabulary or listen to music in Spanish.

(12) Subscribe to a Spanish cable TV channel. Watch the news, soap operas, and sports. Professional broadcasters have superb enunciation and pronunciation, and have an excellent pace of communication that allows you to process information in a context that you are familiar with (i.e. world news, sports, and politics). In contrast, actors in soap operas speak faster and also provide some cultural flavor, as their interactions are interspersed with emotions. Very fascinating!

(13) If you have colleagues in your community mental health agency or school who are Spanish speakers, try to share your lunch with them, establish a relationship and ask them to speak Spanish to you.

(14) The utilization of subliminal messages while sleeping can do wonders for some people. You can set up your recording device and listen to it for an hour as you fall asleep. Sometimes the brain is more receptive of new information when there are fewer distractions. In other words, the information is absorbed effortlessly while you are resting.

(15) Enroll in a conversational Spanish class in your local community college. These courses are inexpensive and have teachers that are well connected to the community activities of Latinos/Hispanics.

(16) Travel abroad and go to non-touristy places. Although places like Cancun are beautiful and relaxing, they rarely provide an opportunity to interact with locals. You can even prearrange some basic conversation classes in Spanish.

(17) Browse Spanish songs on You Tube, especially songs that have the lyrics written and can be followed. This is a fun way of tracking what the artists are saying.

(18) Attend Latino/Hispanic fairs, plays, and festivals. This will allow you to meet interesting people from all sectors of the Latino/Hispanic community.

(19) If you have children, enroll them in Spanish classes as early as you can. Don't wait until they are in junior high to enroll them in classes: start early! Benefit from their learning process and travel the cultural and linguistic journey as a family.

All of these recommendations are what I called *pseudo-immersion activities*. Since you are not living in a Spanish-speaking country, the only way to develop your skills and degree of proficiency is by pseudo-immersing yourself in the Latino/Hispanic culture at home. But remember, you don't have to do all these at once! Use the strategies that best fit your lifestyle, work schedule, and family activities. The idea is to have fun while we learn and not be overwhelmed. One thing is for sure: you will never be the same once you embark on this linguistic and cultural journey!

The sections in this book encased in a box or table and accompanied by the symbols indicate that you will be able to listen to the Spanish phrases, commands or words in Spanish and their respective English translation on the *reader's companion website*. I highly encourage you to listen carefully and repeat the pronunciation aloud in order to refine your skills. Another strategy is to record your pronunciation and compare it with that on the companion website. Don't be afraid to make mistakes! Remember, this is a journey and it goes step by step.

El Alfabeto (*The Alphabet*)

According to the Real Academia de la Lengua Española (The Royal Academy of the Spanish Language) the Spanish alphabet has a total of 27 letters, including the letter Ñ; the CH, LL, and RR have been officially excluded from the alphabet, and are instead used as diagraphs, which are defined as orthographic symbols of two letters. The Spanish alphabet is separated into consonants (*consonantes*) and vowels (*vocales*). The vowels are A, E, I, O, and U, just like in English.

The following table provides you with the letter of the alphabet, an example of a Spanish word to put it in context, and the translation of the word in English:

Letter	Example in Spanish	Translation of Example
A	Ayudar	To help
B	Basta	Stop
C	Cerebro	Brain
D	Dolor	Pain
E	Escuchar	To listen
F	Fácil	Easy
G	Gente	People
H	Humano	Human
I	Irritable	Irritable
J	Trabajar	To work
K	Kilómetro	Kilometer
L	Laboratorio	Laboratory
M	Mentira	A lie
N	Nervioso	Nervous
Ñ	Sueño	Sleep
O	Obesidad	Obesity
P	Parar	To stop
Q	Quejar	To complain
R	Estar	To be
S	Sangre	Blood
T	Tranquilo	Calm, Tranquil
U	Usar	To use
V	Vértigo	Dizzinesss
W	Whiskey	Whiskey
X	Examen	Examination
Y	Inyección	Injection
Z	Zurdo	Left-handed

Vocabulario general que es parecido en inglés y español
(*General Vocabulary That Is Similar in English and Spanish*)

These words mean exactly the same and are written very similarly in both languages. This is an easy way to memorize words by association, rather than in a vacuum!

Accidente	Accident
Aceptar	To Accept
Admitir	To Admit
Analizar	To Analyze
Autorizar	To Authorize
Biológico	Biological
Calmar	To Calm (down)
Caso	Case
Cauteloso/a	Cautious
Cauterizar	To Cauterize
Comprender	To Comprehend
Comunicar	To Communicate
Contaminar	To Contaminate
Decidir	To Decide
Demencia	Dementia
Depender	To Depend (on)
Desinfectar	To Disinfect
Dificultad	Difficulty
Directorio	Directory
Esquizofrénico/a	Schizophrenic
Esterilización	Sterilization
Familia	Family
Físico	Physical
Fracturar	To Fracture
Generoso/a	Generous
Hímen	Hymen
Impotencia	Impotence
Informar	To Inform
Intenso/a	Intense
Intérprete	Interpreter
Inyectar	To Inject
Laboratorio	Laboratory
Mantener	To Maintain
Medicina	Medicine
Mucho	Much

Nervioso/a	Nervous
Neurólogo	Neurologist
Nutrir	To Nurture
Observar	To Observe
Operar	To Operate
Permitir	To Permit
Preparar	To Prepare
Progresar	To Progress
Recomendar	To Recommend
Recuperación	Recuperation
Referir	To Refer
Revivir	To Revive
Sexualidad	Sexuality
Sufrir	To Suffer
Terminar	To Terminate
Termómetro	Thermometer
Transmitir	To Transmit
Usar	To Use
Víctima	Victim
Visitar	To Visit
Vomitar	To Vomit

Acentuación (*Accentuation*)

The aim of this manual is to give you a general understanding of the Spanish language without overwhelming you with the complex mechanics of grammar. Accentuation is broadly defined as the stress or prominence given to certain syllables. Always keep in mind that even though your accentuation may not be the best and may not reach the proficiency level of a native speaker, a person whose first language is Spanish will easily be able to understand what you are trying to say, despite your shortcomings. In Spanish there are only two degrees of stress: strong and weak. For instance:

cli-**en**-te (weak-strong-weak)   con-se-**je**-ro (weak-weak-strong-weak)

There are simple rules for determining the stressed syllable, though keep in mind that not all the stressed syllables bear a written accent. Please don't be overwhelmed by these rules! Normally, as you get to listen to more of the Spanish language, the pronunciation will come automatically by association and context, and not necessarily from a rigid memorization of the rules. Remember that you will not be doing a lot of writing in Spanish, and these are only guidelines if you want to be more technical. The rules are as follows:

(1) A written accent differentiates words (usually monosyllabic) that are spelled the same but have different meanings.

🔊🎧	🔊🎧	*Versus*	🔊🎧	🔊🎧
Dé	give (command)	_	de	from, of
Él	he	_	el	the
Sí	yes	_	si	if
Sé	I know	_	se	himself
Sólo	only	_	solo	Alone (adj)

(2) Questions or interrogative words always have an accent.

🔊🎧	🔊🎧
¿Cómo?	How?
¿Cuál?	Which?
¿Cuándo?	When?
¿Cuánto?	How much?
¿Por qué?	Why?
¿Qué?	What?
¿Quién?	Who?

For the most part, Spanish words do not have a written accent. The following two rules determine where the stressed syllable is:

(a) Words ending in a vowel, -n, or -s stress the next-to-last (penultimate) syllable.

🔊🎧	🔊🎧
Compro (**com**-pro)	I buy
Esta (**es**-ta)	This
Estas (**es**-tas)	These
Limonada (li-mo-**na**-da)	Lemonade

🔊🎧	🔊🎧
Nada (**na**-da)	Nothing
Origen (o-**ri**-gen)	Origin
Zapatos (za-**pa**-tos)	Shoes

(b) Words ending in any consonant except -n or -s are stressed on the last syllable.

🔊🎧	🔊🎧
Ciudad (ci-u-**dad**)	City
Comer (co-**mer**)	To eat
Doctor (doc-**tor**)	Doctor

(c) When rules (a) and (b) above are not followed, a written accent is used.

🔊🎧	🔊🎧
Compró (com-**pró**)	(He, she, they) bought
Está (es-**tá**)	(He, she, it) is
Estás (es-**tás**)	(You) are

¡Practique!

Repita y pronuncie dónde cae el acento de la voz. (*Repeat and pronounce where the vocal accent is placed.*)

🔊🎧	🔊🎧
Consejera	con-se-**je**-ra (counselor)
Conversar	con-ver-**sar** (to talk; formal)
Hablar	ha-**blar** (to talk)
Meditar	me-di-**tar** (to meditate)
Mente	**men**-te (mind)
Preguntar	pre-gun-**tar** (to ask)
Sanar	sa-**nar** (to heal)
Tranquilo/a	tran-**qui**-lo/a (calm, tranquil)

El Tiempo Presente Simple (*The Simple Present Tense*)

The verb *to be* is the most frequently used verb because it can be used to describe a wide range of human aspects and serves as a linguistic framework to express the inner self. There are two versions of this verb in Spanish. The verb *ser* is used to communicate the time, as well as a person's physical and personal characteristics/traits, place of origin, and profession. In contrast, the verb *estar* is normally used in conjunction with the location of things or persons, and with adjectives that describe states of being, such as feelings, physical and mental health, and emotions.

Ser	To be	Estar	To be
Y soy	I am	Yo estoy	I am
Tú eres (*informal*)	You are	Tú estás (*informal*)	You are
Usted es (*formal*)	You are	Usted está (*formal*)	You are
Él/ella es	He/she is	Él/ella está	He/she is
Nosotros somos	We are	Nosotros estamos	We are
Ustedes son (*plural*)	You are	Ustedes están (*plural*)	You are
Ellos/ellas son (*m/f*)	They are	Ellos/ellas están (*m/f*)	They are

Conjugacion de Verbos Regulares en el Presente (*Conjugation of Regular Verbs in the Present*)

All verbs in Spanish end in -**ar**, -**er**, or -**ir**. To conjugate a regular verb you drop the regular -**ar**, -**er**, or -**ir** infinitive ending and add the appropriate verb ending. The following are some examples:

◀))) 🎧 Trabajar	◀))) 🎧 To work
Yo trabajo	I work
Tú trabajas (*informal*)	You work
Usted trabaja (*formal*)	You work
Él/ella trabaja	He/she works
Nosotros trabajamos	We work
Ustedes trabajan (*plural*)	You work
Ellos/ellas trabajan (*m/f*)	They work

🔊🎧 **Atender**	🔊🎧 **To look after**
Yo atiendo	I look after
Tú atiendes *(informal)*	You look after
Usted atiende *(formal)*	You look after
Él/ella atiende	He/she looks after
Nosotros atendemos	We look after
Ustedes atienden *(plural)*	You look after
Ellos/ellas atienden *(m/f)*	They look after

🔊🎧 **Admitir**	🔊🎧 **To admit**
Yo admito	I admit
Tú admites *(informal)*	You admit
Usted admite *(formal)*	You admit
Él/ella admite	He/she admits
Nosotros admitimos	We admit
Ustedes admiten *(plural)*	You admit
Ellos/ellas admiten *(m/f)*	They admit

Conjugacion de Verbos Irregulares en el Tiempo Presente de Indicativo *(Conjugation of Irregular Verbs in the Present Indicative Tense)*

Since these verbs do not follow the regular verb pattern they must be memorized; it is especially helpful to do this in a counseling context to promote cognitive permanence. The following are some examples:

🔊🎧 **Tener**	🔊🎧 **To have**
Yo tengo	I have
Tú tienes *(informal)*	You have
Usted tiene *(formal)*	You have
Él/ella tiene	He/she has
Nosotros tenemos	We have
Ustedes tienen *(plural)*	You have
Ellos/ellas tienen *(m/f)*	They have

◀)) 🎧 **Venir**	◀)) 🎧 **To come**
Yo vengo	I come
Tú vienes *(informal)*	You come
Usted viene *(formal)*	You come
Él/ella viene	He/she comes
Nosotros venimos	We come
Ustedes vienen *(plural)*	You come
Ellos/ellas vienen *(m/f)*	They come

◀)) 🎧 **Ver**	◀)) 🎧 *To see*
Yo veo	I see
Tú ves *(informal)*	You see
Usted ve *(formal)*	You see
Él/ella ve	He/she sees
Nosotros vemos	We see
Ustedes ven *(plural)*	You see
Ellos/ellas ven *(m/f)*	They see

Los Verbos "Ponerse" (*To Become/Get*) y "Sentirse" (*To Feel*)

These verbs are typically associated and used when referring to feelings. They are conjugated in the present time. There are many ways of expressing feelings and sometimes one word is sufficient. These verbs, however, can stress the intensity of these feelings.

◀)) 🎧 **Poner (se)**	◀)) 🎧 **To become/get**
Yo me pongo	I become/get
Tú te pones *(informal)*	You become/get
Usted se pone *(formal)*	You become/get
Él/ella se pone	He/she becomes/gets
Nosotros nos ponemos	We become/get
Ustedes se ponen *(plural)*	You become/get
Ellos/ellas se ponen *(m/f)*	They become/get

◀))) 🎧 **Sentir (se)**	◀))) 🎧 **To feel**
Yo me siento	I feel
Tú te sientes *(informal)*	You feel
Usted se siente *(formal)*	You feel
Él/ella se siente	He/she feels
Ustedes se sienten *(plural)*	You feel
Nosotros nos sentimos	We feel
Ellos/ellas se sienten *(m/f)*	They feel

◀))) 🎧 **Ejemplos usando poner (se) y sentir (se)**	◀))) 🎧 **Examples using to become/get and to feel**
Yo me pongo triste con las situaciones.	I become sad about situations.
Tú te pones frustrado con los problemas.	You (informal) get frustrated with problems.
Ella se siente ansiosa en lugares nuevos.	She feels anxious in new places.
Nosotros nos sentimos alegres con tus éxitos.	We feel happy with your. achievements
Ustedes se ponen de mal humor cuando toman cerveza.	You (formal, plural) get in a bad mood when you drink beer.
Ellos se ponen furiosos cuando el jefe los regaña.	They get angry when their boss reprimands them.
Yo me siento agobiado.	I feel overwhelmed.
Tú te sientes deprimida.	You (informal) feel depressed.
Ustedes se sienten bien después de la sesión de consejería.	You (formal, plural) feel good after the counseling session.
Ellas se sienten bien cada vez que hablan con usted.	They (feminine, plural) feel good every time they talk with you.

Dos Tiempos para el Pasado en Español: Pretérito e Imperfecto (*Two Past Tenses in Spanish: Preterite and Imperfect*)

The preterite and the imperfect are tenses that express a past action. In essence, the preterite expresses the beginning, end, or completion of an action. It also describes a specific action within a definite time period in the past.

Verbos Regulares del Tiempo Pretérito (Regular Verbs of the Preterite)

🔊 Ayudar	🔊 To help
Yo ayudé	I helped
Tú ayudaste *(informal)*	You helped
Usted ayudó *(formal)*	You helped
Él/ella ayudó	He/she helped
Nosotros ayudamos	We helped
Ustedes ayudaron *(plural)*	You helped
Ellos/ellas ayudaron *(m/f)*	They helped

🔊 Temer	🔊 To fear
Yo temí	I feared
Tú temiste *(informal)*	You feared
Usted temió *(formal)*	You feared
Él/ella temió	He/she feared
Nosotros temimos	We feared
Ustedes temieron *(plural)*	You feared
Ellos/ellas temieron *(m/f)*	They feared

🔊 Sentir	🔊 To feel
Yo sentí	I felt
Tú sentiste *(informal)*	You felt
Usted sintió *(formal)*	You felt
Él/ella sintió	He/she felt
Nosotros sentimos	We felt
Ustedes sintieron *(plural)*	You felt
Ellos/ellas sintieron *(m/f)*	They felt

Verbos Irregulares del Pretérito (Irregular Verbs of the Preterite)

Ser	To be	Estár	To be	Tener	To have
Yo fui	I was	Yo estuve	I was	Yo tuve	I had
Tú fuiste (informal)	You were	Tú estuviste (informal)	You were	Tú tuviste (informal)	You had
Usted fue (formal)	You were	Usted estuvo (formal)	You were	Usted tuvo (formal)	You had
Él/ella fue	He/she was	Él/ella estuvo	He/she was	Él/ella tuvo	He/she had
Nosotros fuimos	We were	Nosotros estuvimos	We were	Nosotros tuvimos	We had
Ustedes fueron (plural)	You were	Ustedes estuvieron (plural)	You were	Ustedes tuvieron (plural)	You had
Ellos/ellas fueron (m/f)	They were	Ellos/ellas estuvieron (m/f)	They were	Ellos/ellas tuvieron (m/f)	They had

The imperfect tense is the second important tense that expresses action in the past. It is used for telling time in the past, expressing how things used to be, talking about what is going on, and describing persons or things in the past. The following are three illustrations of the imperfect tense.

Verbos regulares del tiempo imperfecto (Regular Verbs of the Imperfect Tense)

Leer	To read
Yo leía	I used to read
Tú leías (informal)	You used to read
Usted leía (formal)	You used to read
Él/ella leía	He/she used to read
Nosotros leíamos	We used to read
Ustedes leían (formal)	You used to read
Ellos/ellas leían (m/f)	They used to read

Abrazar	To hug
Yo abrazaba	I used to hug
Tú abrazabas *(informal)*	You used to hug
Usted abrazaba *(formal)*	You used to hug
Él/ella abrazaba	He/she used to hug
Nosotros abrazábamos	We used to hug
Ustedes abrazaban *(plural)*	You used to hug
Ellos/ellas abrazaban *(m/f)*	They used to hug

Escuchar	To listen
Yo escuchaba	I used to listen
Tú escuchabas *(informal)*	You used to listen
Usted escuchaba *(formal)*	You used to listen
Él/ella escuchaba	He/she used to listen
Nosotros escuchabamos	We used to listen
Ustedes escuchaban *(plural)*	You used to listen
Ellos/ellas escuchaban *(m/f)*	They used to listen

Verbos irregulares del tiempo imperfecto (*Irregular Verbs of the Imperfect Tense*)

Remember that "ser" is an irregular verb in the imperfect. Here you will find the conjugation of this verb as well as "estar" and "tener," which are used frequently.

Ser	To be	Estar	To be	Tener	To have
Yo era	I used to be/was	Yo estaba	I used to be/was	Yo tenía	I used to have/had
Tú eras *(informal)*	You used to be/were	Tú estabas *(informal)*	You used to be/were	Tú tenías *(informal)*	You used to have/had
Usted era *(formal)*	You used to be/were	Usted estaba *(formal)*	You used to be/were	Usted tenía *(formal)*	You used to have/had
Él/ella era	He/she used to be/was	Él/ella estaba	He/she used to be/was	Él/ella tenía	He/she used to have/had

Ser	To be	Estar	To be	Tener	To have
Nosotros éramos	We used to be/were	Nosotros estábamos	We used to be/were	Nosotros teníamos	We used to have/had
Ustedes eran *(plural)*	You used to be/were	Ustedes estaban *(plural)*	You used to be/were	Ustedes tenían *(plural)*	You used to have/had
Ellos/ellas eran *(m/f)*	They used to be/were	Ellos/ellas estaban *(m/f)*	They used to be/were	Ellos/ellas tenían *(m/f)*	They used to have/had

Los Números (*Numbers*)

Numbers are instrumental in any conversation because they provide a sense of direction, weight, distance, magnitude, space, time, and consequence. Once you know numbers in Spanish and they are put in context by the unit (e.g., feet, ounces, hours, etc.), the conversation has direction. Sometimes you do not have to construct a full sentence as long as you know the number and unit. Normally, the other person will fill in the blanks. The following are the cardinal numbers:

Números Cardinales (*Cardinal Numbers*)	
0	Cero
1	Uno
2	Dos
3	Tres
4	Cuatro
5	Cinco
6	Seis
7	Siete
8	Ocho
9	Nueve
10	Diez
11	Once
12	Doce
13	Trece
14	Catorce
15	Quince
16	Dieciséis

17	Diecisiete
18	Dieciocho
19	Diecinueve
20	Veinte
21	Veintiuno
22	Veintidos
30	Treinta
33	Treinta y tres
40	Cuarenta
44	Cuarenta y cuatro
50	Cincuenta
55	Cincuenta y cinco
60	Sesenta
66	Sesenta y seis
70	Setenta
77	Setenta y siete
80	Ochenta
88	Ochenta y ocho
90	Noventa
99	Noventa y nueve
100	Cien
101	Ciento uno
200	Doscientos
202	Doescientos dos
300	Trescientos
303	Trescientos tres
400	Cuatrocientos
404	Cuatrocientos cuatro
500	Quinientos
505	Quinientos cinco
600	Seiscientos
606	Seiscientos seis
700	Setecientos
707	Setecientos siete
800	Ochocientos

Números Cardinales (Cardinal Numbers)	
808	Ochocientos ocho
900	Novecientos
909	Novecientos nueve
1,000	Mil
1,910	Mil novecientos diez
1,966	Mil novecientos sesenta y seis
2,000	Dos mil
2,212	Dos mil doscientos doce
6,000	Seis mil
6,016	Seis mil dieciséis
8,000	Ocho mil
8,188	Ocho mil ciento ochenta y ocho
1,000,000	Un millón

In general, cardinal numbers have the same form no matter how they are used. However, *uno* and multiples of *ciento* agree in number and gender with the nouns that they are modifying. When you drop the final syllable-*to* and are left with *cien* from the original *ciento*, it can be placed before a masculine or feminine noun. Also, *uno* drops the-*o* preceding a masculine noun and changes -*o* to -*a* preeceding a feminine noun.

Algunos ejemplos	Some examples
Un asunto	An issue
Cien dólares	One hundred dollars
Una cita	Appointment
Un cliente	Client
Un consejero	Counselor (male)
Una consejera	Counselor (female)
Un frasco	Bottle
Un hombre	Man
Una mujer	Woman
Una pastilla	Pill
Un problema	Problem
Una sesión	Session
Una situación	Situation

Ordinal numbers become handy when it comes to providing position, distance, and time. Read the translations and listen to the pronunciation of these examples.

🔊🎧 Números ordinales	🔊🎧 Ordinal numbers
Primero	First
Segundo	Second
Tercero	Third
Cuarto	Fourth
Quinto	Fifth
Sexto	Sixth
Séptimo	Seventh
Octavo	Eight
Noveno	Ninth
Décimo	Tenth

🔊🎧 Ejemplos usando números ordinales	🔊🎧 Examples using ordinal numbers
El cuarto incidente	The fourth incident
La decima persona	The tenth person
La novena cita	The ninth appointment
La octava situación	The eigth situation
El primer cliente	The first client
La segunda factura	The second bill
El séptimo grupo	The seventh group
La sexta página	The sixth page
La tercera alucinación	The third hallucination
La quinta intervención	The fifth intervention

Meses, dias, y estaciones (*Months, Days, and Seasons*)

🔊🎧 Los Meses del Año	🔊🎧 The Months of the Year
enero	January
febrero	February
marzo	March
abril	April

🔊🎧 Los Meses del Año	🔊🎧 The Months of the Year
mayo	May
junio	June
julio	July
agosto	August
septiembre	September
octubre	October
noviembre	November
diciembre	December

🔊🎧 Los Días de la Semana	🔊🎧 The Days of the Week
El domingo	Sunday
El lunes	Monday
El martes	Tuesday
El miércoles	Wednesday
El jueves	Thursday
El viernes	Friday
El sábado	Saturday

🔊🎧 Las Estaciones del Año	🔊🎧 The Seasons of the Year
El invierno	Winter
El otoño	Fall/autumn
La primavera	Spring
El verano	Summer

Note: Do not capitalize Spanish months, days, or seasons.

🔊🎧 Vocabulario Adicional sobre la Fecha/la Hora	🔊🎧 Additional Date/Time Vocabulary
Año	Year
Año bisiesto	Leap year
Año económico	Fiscal year
Año escolar	School year

Calendario	Calendar
Día	Day
Día de fiesta, día festivo	Holiday
Fecha	Date
Fin de semana	Weekend
Hora	Hour
Hora de verano	Daylight saving time
Hora normal/hora legal	Standard time
Media noche	Midnight
Mediodía	Noon
Minuto	Minute
Navidad	Christmas
Nochebuena	Christmas Eve
Pascua (de Resurrección)	Easter
Semana	Week
Víspera de año nuevo	New Year's Eve

¡Practique!

¿Qué hora es?	Es la una. *(It is one o'clock.)*
	Son las dos. *(It is two o'clock.)*
	Son las tres y cuarto. *(It is a quarter after three.)*
	Son las cuatro y media. *(It is half past four.)*
	Son las cinco y cuarenta y cinco. *(It is five forty-five.)*
	Son las seis menos cuarto. *(It is a quarter to six.)*
	Son las siete menos diez. *(It is ten to seven.)*

Otras Expresiones que Denotan Tiempo	**Other Expressions of Time**
A eso de…	At about…
Ahora	Now
A las…	At…
Al despertarse	Upon waking up
Al levantarse	Upon getting up
Al mediodía	At noon
A media noche	At midnight
Antes de la comida/antes de comer	Before meals
Después de la comida/después de comer	After meals

Otras Expresiones que Denotan Tiempo	***Other Expressions of Time***
Anualmente	Yearly
A veces	Sometimes
Ayer	Yesterday
Cada hora	Every hour
Cada minuto	Every minute
La madrugada	Morning (between midnight and sunrise)
La mañana	Morning (between sunrise and noon)
La tarde	Afternoon (between noon and sunset)
La noche	Night (between sunset and midnight)
Diario, diariamente	Daily
Durante el día	During the day
Durante la noche	During the night
El mes que viene	Next month
En punto	Exactly/o'clock
En unos minutos, dentro de poco	In a few minutes, shortly
Esta noche	Tonight
Hace poco	A short while ago
Hoy	Today
Por ahora	As of now
Para esa fecha	By that date
Por día, cada día	Per day
Por muchos años	For many years
Por muchos días	For many days
Por muchos meses	For many months
¿Por cuánto tiempo?	For how long?
Primera vez	First time
La semana que viene	Next week
La última vez	Last time
Mañana	Tomorrow
Mensualmente	Monthly
Todo el año	Year round
Últimamente	Lately
Una semana a partir de hoy	A week from today
Una vez al día	Once a day

Países y Nacionalidades (*Countries and Nationalities*)

◀))) ∩ País, Nacionalidad	◀))) ∩ Country, Nationality
Cuba, cubano/a	Cuba, Cuban
Puerto Rico, puertorriqueño/a	Puerto Rico, Puerto Rican
La República Dominicana, dominicano/a	The Dominican Republic, Dominican
Argentina, argentino/a	Argentina, Argentinian
Uruguay, uruguayo/a	Uruguay, Uruguayan
Chile, chileno/a	Chile, Chilean
Paraguay, paraguayo/a	Paraguay, Paraguayan
Bolivia, boliviano/a	Bolivia, Bolivian
Perú, peruano/a	Peru, Peruvian
Ecuador, ecuatoriano/a	Ecuador, Ecuadorian
Colombia, colombiano/a	Colombia, Colombian
Venezuela, venezolano/a	Venezuela, Venezuelan
Panamá, panameño/a	Panama, Panamanian
Costa Rica, costarricense	Costa Rica, Costa Rican
Nicaragua, nicaragüense	Nicaragua, Nicaraguan
El Salvador, salvadoreño/a	El Salvador, Salvadorian
Honduras, hondureño/a	Honduras, Honduran
Guatemala, guatemalteco/a	Guatemala, Guatemalan
México, mexicano/a	Mexico, Mexican
Los Estados Unidos, americano/a, estadounidense	United States, (North) American
España, español (a)	Spain, Spaniard

Fracciones, decimales, y dimensiones (*Fractions, Decimals, and Dimensions*)

◀))) ∩ Fracciones	◀))) ∩ Fractions
1/4 un cuarto, la cuarta parte	One fourth, a quarter
1/3 un tercio, la tercera parte	One third, a third
1/2 un medio, la mitad	One half, half
2/3 dos tercios	Two thirds
3/4 tres cuartos	Three fourths/quarters
1½ uno/a y medio/a	One and a half

🔊🎧 Decimales	🔊🎧 Decimals
Unidades	Units
Décimas	Tenths
Centésimas	Hundredths
Milésimas	Thousandths

🔊🎧 Dimensiones (Nombres)	🔊🎧 Dimensions (Nouns)
La altura (estatura)	Height
La anchura	Width
El espesor	Thickness
La longitud	Length
La profundidad	Depth

🔊🎧 Dimensiones (Adjetivos)	🔊🎧 Dimensions (Adjectives)
Alto	Tall
Ancho	Wide
Grueso	Thick
Largo	Long
Profundo	Deep

Working with Vocabulary and Integration of Concepts

You can combine these words to create short sentences, commands, or phrases. The following are possible combinations that can be very handy when you need to ask basic questions in an initial conversation or if you need to find out further information.

¡Practique!

Escuche atentamente la pregunta o afirmación. *(Listen carefully to the question or statement.)*	Repita en español. *(Repeat in Spanish.)*
1. Counselor: What time is my appointment? Client: At twelve o'clock.	Consejero: ¿A qué hora es mi cita? Cliente: A las doce en punto (12:00).
2. Counselor: How long have you felt depressed? Client: For many months.	Consejero: ¿Por cuánto tiempo se ha sentido deprimido? Cliente: Por muchos meses.
4. Counselor: Your next appointment is next month. Client: Thank you.	Consejero: Su próxima cita es el mes que viene. Cliente: Gracias.
5. Counselor: When do you feel worst? Client: At night.	Consejero: ¿Cuándo se siente peor? Cliente: Por la noche.
6. Counselor: The fifth appointment is on Wednesday.	Consejero: La quinta cita es el miércoles.
7. Who would you like to talk to?	¿Con quién le gustaría hablar?
8. There is a group session tonight.	Esta noche hay una sesión de grupo.
9. We will finish in a few minutes.	Terminaremos en unos minutos.
10. Counselor: What happened last summer? Client: I divorced my husband.	Consejero: ¿Qué pasó el verano pasado? Cliente: Me divorcié de mi esposo.
11. Counselor: When do you see your family? Client: At Christmas.	Consejero: ¿Cuándo ve a su familia? Cliente: Por navidad.
12. Counselor: When do you feel better? Client: In the summer.	Consejero: ¿Cuándo se siente mejor? Cliente: En el verano.

4 Counselors, Social Workers, and Psychologists

Mental Health, Latinos/Hispanics, and Discrimination

According to some research studies, the perceived discrimination among Latinos/Hispanics has a negative impact on income levels, academic achievement, opportunities in life, and ultimately on their mental health outcomes (Noh & Kasper, 2003). Those who have indicated they have been victims of discrimination present higher levels of stress and depression, and have poor mental health compared to those who have not perceived, experienced, or reported it (Taylor & Turner, 2002). According to one survey, 83 percent of all Latinos/Hispanics interviewed reported that discrimination against them is a problem (Pew Hispanic Center/Kaiser Family Foundation, 2002). This survey also showed that 41 percent of all Latinos/Hispanics interviewed reported receiving poorer service in restaurants and stores, 30 percent had been called names or insulted, and 14 percent had not been hired or promoted because of racial and/or cultural discrimination (Pew Hispanic Center/Kaiser Family Foundation, 2002).

It seems that Latino/Hispanic discrimination appears to be mostly attributed to their racial and ethnic status, and on their physical appearance (i.e. skin color) for those who have a darker complexion. Having limited fluency in the English language and a thick accent appear to exacerbate discriminatory experiences. As indicated in Chapter One, the Latino/Hispanic community disagrees on a single definition of itself. This is evidenced by the difficulties experienced by the US Federal Census Bureau in racially classifying Latinos/Hispanics. Over half (approximately 53 percent) of Latinos/Hispanics identified themselves as White Hispanic, 2 percent identified themselves as Black Hispanic, 1 percent Native Indian Hispanic, 0.4 percent Asian Hispanic, and 39 percent identified themselves as Some Other Race (US Census Bureau, 2010).

Based on these statistics, darker-skinned Latinos/Hispanics report that they experience discrimination in their daily lives and occupational settings, especially when they are searching for employment (Logan, 2004). In contrast, lighter-skinned Latino/Hispanic immigrants such as Cubans, Puerto Ricans, and South Americans have greater success educationally and occupationally than their fellow countrymen who have darker skin (Araújo & Borrell, 2006). Interestingly, although one would assume that the source of racism and discrimination would be coming from those of European American (Anglo) descent, there are reports of intra-ethnic racism, among members of the same nationality and ethnic group (Taylor & Turner, 2002). From a gender standpoint, Latino/Hispanic women report fewer incidents of racism, prejudice, and discrimination in their workplace and daily lives. It is assumed that the majority of Latino/Hispanic women have developed strong coping skills and a tight support network among themselves in a male-dominated culture, which results in them being able to adjust better when facing adversity (Noh & Kasper, 2003; Taylor & Turner, 2002). Understanding the racial and ethnic environment that Latinos/Hispanics have to navigate on a daily basis is critical. In addition to the cultural and linguistic nuances that they bring with them, they are also carrying a lot of emotional baggage relative to their prejudice and discrimination experiences. Therefore, it is critical to understand the phenomenological and anecdotal experiences of Latino/Hispanic clients when they come to your office for the first time.

Registering at Reception

The First Contact

The outcome of the counseling process or a case management interview will start to be determined with the very first contact the client makes either with an office staff member at the registration desk or with us mental health providers. Therefore, it is critically important to send an unequivocal message that we are culturally sensitive, not just by knowing about the Latino/Hispanic culture but by demonstrating that we have invested time and energy as students of the Spanish language. If you feel embarrassed because of your limited Spanish language skills, accent, or mispronunciation, remember that our Spanish-speaking clients are in need of help. Therefore, if they do not speak English well they will be extremely grateful for your efforts, as they are the ones who feel they are in a disadvantaged position for not speaking the dominant language. As a result, they will not correct your grammar and pronunciation – they will thank you!

Cultural hints: Latinos/Hispanics believe in *respeto* (respect). They will hold you in high regard for being a professional and will address you as *Señor* (Mr.), *Señora* (Mrs./Ms.), or *Doctor* (Dr.). Do not encourage them to address you by your first name unless you have worked with them for a prolonged period of time. Acknowledging professionals by their first names may be seen as disrespectful and takes away your credibility as a professional. Bicultural or more acculturated individuals may not hold these beliefs and will operate within the same parameters as the dominant culture.

Saludos (Greetings)

As in US culture, a handshake is the best way to greet Latinos/Hispanics. The difference is that the handshake is perhaps not as firm as in US American culture. Be they adults, youths, or children, most Latinos/Hispanics are used to a handshake as a sign of politeness, courtesy, and good manners.

Cultural hints: Keep in mind that prolonged eye contact is not the norm in Latino/Hispanic culture. It is perhaps somewhat disrespectful to keep eye contact, especially among children and youth. They will avoid it, although it is not necessarily a sign of being shy, timid, or resistant to treatment. Again, there are variations among Latino/Hispanic populations. Individuals with a stronger European cosmopolitan background are accustomed to direct eye contact and assertive communication.

¡Practique!

Saludos	Greetings
Buenos días	Good morning
Buenas tardes. ¿Cómo está, señor Pérez?	Good afternoon. How are you, Mr. Pérez?
Buenas noches. ¿Cómo está, señora Rodríguez?	Good evening. How are you, Mrs. Rodríguez?
Hola	Hello/Hi

¡Practique!

Despedidas	Farewells
Adiós	Goodbye
Buenas noches	Good night
Espero verlo de nuevo	I hope to see you again
Hasta mañana	See you tomorrow
Nos vemos después	See you later
Nos vemos pronto	See you soon
Que tenga un buen día	Have a nice day

Cultural hints: Avoid calling your client's name out loud like in a physician's office. Being in a counselor's office is shameful enough for many Latino/Hispanic clients, who see their visit as a personal defeat or weakness. They would like to keep the counseling process as private as it can be. Consequently, either you or your office staff should approach the clients quietly and encourage them either to come in or complete the intake forms without drawing the attention of others.

Useful Nouns during Registration

You will be amazed to see what the use of a simple noun in conjunction with non-verbal gestures can do for you! For example, how many times have we waved to a server in a restaurant and gesticulated in the air as if we were writing to indicate that we want the check or pointed at the glass assuming that the server knows that we want a refill? The same principle applies to this type of linguistic interaction. If you run out of prepositions or connecting words, non-verbal gestures will fill the spaces wonderfully. Let's start with a list of the most used nouns at a registration desk.

¡Practique!

Nombres	Nouns
La alergía	Allergy
El apellido	Last name
El asiento	Seat
La consejera	Counselor (female)
El consejero	Counselor (male)
De	Of (indicates possession)
El dinero/la plata	Money
La doctora	Doctor (female)
El doctor	Doctor (male)
La enferma	Sick woman/girl
El enfermo	Sick man/boy
La esposa	Wife
El esposo	Husband
La fecha de nacimiento	Date of birth
El formulario	Form
La hija	Daughter
El hijo	Son
La identificación	Identification
El lápiz	Pencil
La licencia de conducir/manejar	Driver's license
El lugar de nacimiento	Place of birth
La madre/mamá	Mother
El mostrador	Counter
La nacionalidad	Nationality
El nombre	Name

La oficina	Office
El padre/papá	Father
La pluma/bolígrafo	Pen
La psicóloga	Psychologist (female)
El psicólogo	Psychologist (male)
La ropa	Clothing
La sala de espera	Waiting room
La secretaria	Secretary (female)
El secretario	Secretary (male)
El seguro/la aseguranza	Insurance
El segundo nombre	Middle name
La señora	Lady
El señor	Gentleman
El sofa	Sofa
La trabajadora social	Social worker (female)
El trabajador social	Social worker (male)

Remember the feminine (*La*) and masculine (*El*) definite articles. If you suddenly forget the correct feminine or masculine definite articles simply use the noun with a slight interrogative tone, for example, *¿Formulario?* (Form?). This sends the message.

Cultural hints: Many Latinos/Hispanics use their hands to emphasize a point of view or to give more intensity to their words. Therefore, using your hands to compensate for a lack of Spanish vocabulary will not be seen as something rude.

Useful Verbs

As you already know, verbs imply action! The combination of nouns and verbs in conjunction with non-verbal gestures will allow you to give basic commands and instructions to your Spanish-speaking clients. These are some of the most commonly used verbs at the registration desk:

¡Practique!

Verbos	Verbs
Empezar	To start
Entender	To understand
Entrar	To come in

Enviar	To send
Escribir	To write
Esperar	To wait
Estar	To be (in a certain place)
Firmar	To sign
Ir a	To go to
Llegar	To arrive
Llenar	To fill in (a form)
Pagar	To pay
Pensar	To think
Perdonar	To forgive/apologize
Presentar	To introduce
Proveer	To provide/give
Refleccionar	To reflect
Registrar	To register
Salir	To leave
Ser	To be (personal characteristic)
Tener	To have
Terminar	To finish
Ver	To see
Venir	To come

Questions and Linguistic Expressions

The following are some basic questions and expressions that will allow you to start a conversation and obtain information, or at least give you an idea about the needs of the clients at the registration desk.

¡Practique!

Preguntas/Frases	Questions/Phrases
¿A qué hora?	At what time?
Adiós	Good bye
Aquí está, aquí está …	Here it is/here is …
Cancelar	To cancel
¿Cuál es su nombre?	What is your name?
Confirmar	To confirm

¿Cuál es su ...?	Which is your ...?
Cuídese *(formal)*, Cuídate *(informal)*	Take care
Dar	To give
Por nada	You are welcome
El dinero	Money
Dinero en efectivo	Cash
Él/ella le atenderá en un momento	He/she will be with you in a moment
Encontrará ...	You will find ...
¿Entiende?	Do you understand?
Espere aquí, por favor	Wait here, please
¿Es residente?	Are you a resident?
¿Es una emergencia?	Is it an emergency?
¿Está listo/a?	Are you ready?
Gracias	Thank you
Hable despacio, por favor	Speak slowly, please
Hasta luego	I will see you later
Hoja de referido	Referral form
Horas de oficina	Office hours
Le quiero ayudar	I want to help you
Llegar tarde	To be late
Mi	My
Mi nombre es ...	My name is ...
Yo necesito ...	I need ...
El necesita ...	He needs ...
Ella necesita ...	She needs ...
Ellos necesitan ...	They need ...
No	No
Por favor	Please
¿Preguntas?	Questions?
El problema	Problem
Quizás	Maybe
¿Qué desea usted?	What do you need?
Responsable	Responsible
Ser puntual	To be on time

Sí	Yes
Siéntese aquí, por favor	Sit here, please
Siga las instrucciones	Follow the instructions
La situación	The situation
Su	Your/his/her
Tarjeta de crédito	Credit card
¿Tiene documentos?	Do you have documents?
Tiene que …	You have to …
¿Él tiene …?	Does he have …?
¿Ella tiene …?	Does she have …?
¿Usted tiene …?	Do you have …?
Venga …	Come …
Mi nombre es …	My name is …
¿Cómo le puedo ayudar? ¿En qué le puedo servir?	How can I help you?

So, it is now time to integrate all the new words that you have been learning and put them in a counseling context! Keep in mind that words memorized in isolation will be forgotten quickly. *In order to retain their meaning and pronunciation you have to put yourself in a counseling context.* In this way, the words will make sense and will be learned and stored in your mind by *association*. Do not feel intimidated by all the new concepts and words. Just experience the freedom of trying something new without being evaluated! This is your own journey as a professional, adult learner.

Working with Vocabulary and the Integration of Concepts

Combine some words to create short sentences, commands, or phrases. The following are possible combinations that can be very handy during the first contact with clients at the registration desk:

¡Practique!

1. **Necesita …**	firmar el formulario
	esperar aquí
	pagar
	ir a la oficina
	ver el consejero

conseguir el documento

venir mañana

llamar por la tarde

llamar a la secretaria

llamar a su trabajo

más consejería

2. **Necesito ...**   pagar en la oficina

su licencia de conducir

su firma

la forma de referido

el documento

su fecha de nacimiento

más información

que hable despacio, por favor

su cooperación

su atención, por favor

3. **Tiene que ...**   firmar

llenar el formulario

ir al baño

escribir el nombre de su esposo

incluir la firma de su esposa

esperar un momento

llamar a su jefe

llamar a su familia

seguir las instrucciones

traer los documentos

volver mañana

4. ¿Tiene ...	su licencia?
	una identificación?
	familiares?
	instrucciones?
	una emergencia?
	cheques?
	dinero en efectivo?
	más preguntas?

5. ¿Cuál es ...	su esposo/a?
	el formulario?
	su hijo/a?
	su nacionalidad?
	el documento?
	su pregunta?
	el/la cliente?
	la situación?
	el problema?

Basic Interactive Dialogues at the Registration Desk

¡Practique!

Case Study 1: Don Rodrigo

Counseling context: Don Rodrigo arrives at the office and speaks Spanish to your administrative assistant. She calls you and indicates that she does not understand what he is trying to say. You (the counselor) approach him ... *(Don Rodrigo llega a su oficina y le habla español a su asistente administrativa. Ella le llama a usted y le indica que no entiende lo que él le está tratando de decir. Usted (la consejera) se acerca a él ...)*

Don Rodrigo:	¿Habla usted español? *(Do you speak Spanish?)*
Counselor:	Sí, un poco. ¿En qué le puedo servir? (*Yes, a little bit. How can I help you?*)
Don Rodrigo:	Este es un documento de la corte que el juez me dió indicando que tenía que verla a usted. *(This is a document from the court that the judge gave me indicating that I had to see you.)*
Counselor:	¿Puedo verlo por favor? *(Can I see it please?)*
Don Rodrigo:	Sí, claro. *(Yes, of course.)*
Counselor:	Este documento dice que usted tiene que ver un consejero unas siete veces. *(This document says that you have to see a counselor seven times.)*
Don Rodrigo:	Yo le dije al juez que yo no estaba loco y que no necesitaba ver a nadie ... *(I told the judge that I was not crazy and that I didn't need to see anyone.)*
Counselor:	Nadie ha dicho que usted está loco. Esto es una oportunidad para hablar de la situación sobre su familia. *(Nobody has said that you are crazy. This is just an opportunity to talk about your family situation.)*
Don Rodrigo:	Está bien. *(All right.)*
Counselor:	Por favor, ¿podría completar estas formas? *(Please, can you complete these forms?)*

¡Practique!

Case Study 2: Marta

Counseling context: Marta arrives at the office and speaks Spanish to your administrative assistant. She calls you and indicates that she does not understand what Marta is trying to say. You (the counselor) approach her ... *(Marta llega a su oficina y le habla español a su asistente administrativa. Ella le llama a usted y le indica que no entiende lo que Marta le está tratando de decir. Usted (el/laconsejero/a) se acerca a ellos ...).*

Marta:	¿Habla usted español? *(Do you speak Spanish?)*
Counselor:	Sí, un poco. ¿En qué le puedo servir? (*Yes, a little bit. How can I help you?*)
Marta:	Yo hablo un poco de inglés. Lo que pasa es que me da vergüenza pues no lo sé pronunciar muy bien. (*I speak a little bit of English. The problem is that I feel embarrassed because I don't know how to pronounce it very well.*)

Counselor: Entonces estamos igual. ¡Mi español no es muy bueno tampoco! *(Then we are the same. My Spanish is not very good either!)*

Marta: Muy bien, muy bien [riéndose]. Mi hermana me dijo que viniera aquí porque dijo que alguien me podía ayudar. Últimamente no puedo dormir, me da por llorar sin motivo, y me siento muy triste. *(All right, all right [laughing]. My sister told me to come here because she said that somebody could help me. Lately, I have been unable to sleep, I start crying for no reason, and I feel very sad.)*

Counselor: Vamos adentro. No se preocupe, aquí la vamos a ayudar. *(Let's go inside. Don't worry, we will help you here.)*

¡Practique!

Case Study 3: Jaime and Maritza

Counseling context: Jaime and Maritza arrive at the office speaking broken Spanish and English to your administrative assistant. She calls you and indicates that she is having a hard time following their conversation. You (the counselor) approached them … *(Jaime y Maritza llegan a su oficina hablándole inglés y español a medias a su asistente administrativa. Ella le llama y le indica que lo está pasando difícil al tratar de seguir la conversación. Usted (el/laconsejero/a) se acerca a ellos …)*

Maritza: Buenas tardes. Estoy aquí con Jaime (mi esposo) pues esta es la última oportunidad que le doy para salvar nuestro matrimonio. Yo le dije que si … *(Good afternoon. I am here with Jaime (my husband) because this is the last chance I am giving him to save our marriage.)*

Jaime: Yo no sé si esto va a funcionar. No creo que la culpa sea mía. *(I don't know if this is going to work. I don't think this is my fault.)*

Counselor: Todo esto es muy importante y privado. ¿Quisieran entrar conmigo a la oficina? Mi español es regular pero quizás les puedo ayudar. Síganme, por favor. *(All this is very important and private. Would you like to come with me to the office? My Spanish is so-so but perhaps I can help you both. Follow me, please.)*

The Intake Interview

The intake interview or evaluation session is a multipurpose session. It allows the counselor to complete an evaluation, render a diagnosis, or submit a referral. Due to the importance of the intake interview – and since it involves a diagnosis and a treatment plan – it must only be conducted by counselors who have a high level of Spanish proficiency or who are under the supervision of a counselor who does. This section provides both brief and in-depth versions of intake interviews. Both of them are contained on the *reader's companion website* so you can hear the correct pronunciation.

An In-Depth Life History Questionnaire for an Intake Interview

The following is a sample of a life history questionnaire form that can be completed by the clients, assuming that they have a basic level of literacy in Spanish. For instructional purposes, an English translation is provided in parentheses and italics; however, it may be a good idea to keep this bilingual version for clients who have different levels of language proficiency and can complement their linguistic deficiencies by reading certain concepts and terminologies in both languages. Of course, you also have the option of utilizing only the pertinent questions that you want to emphasize, and not necessarily the entire questionnaire.

Cuestionario del Historial Vivencial *(Life History Questionnaire)*
El propósito de este cuestionario es obtener información general de su vida, experiencia, y trasfondo cultural/social. Al completar este cuestionario de la forma más detallada permitirá al profesional desarrollar un mejor plan de ayuda de acuerdo a sus necesidades específicas. Por favor devuelva este cuestionario a la asistente administrativa o al momento de su cita de consejería. *(The purpose of this questionnaire is to obtain general information about your life, experience, and cultural/social background. Completing this questionnaire in as much detailas possible will allow the counselor to develop a better plan to help you according to your specific needs. Please return this questionnaire to the administrative assistant or at your counseling appointment.)*

Por favor conteste las siguientes preguntas *(Please answer the following questions)*

Fecha *(Date)* _____
Nombre *(Name)* _____
Dirección *(Address)* _____
_____
_____
Número telefónico de día *(Daytime telephone number)* _____
Número telefónico de noche *(Evening telephone number)* _____
Fecha de nacimiento *(Date of birth)* _____
Edad *(Age)* _____
Ocupación *(Occupation)* _____
¿Por quién fue referido? *(By whom were you referred?)* _____

¿Con quién reside actualmente? Haga una lista de personas. *(With whom are you currently living? Make a list of people.)*

¿Dónde reside? *(Where do you live?)* ____casa *(house)*____hotel *(hotel)* ___cuarto *(room)* ___apartamento *(apartment)* ___otro *(other)*

Estado civil *(Civil status)*

__ soltero/a *(single)*

__ comprometido/a *(engaged)*

__ casado/a *(married)*

__ divorciado/a *(divorced)*

__segundo o tercer matrimonio *(second or third marriage)*

__relación estable con una persona *(in a stable relationship)*

__viudo/a *(widowed)*

Nombre, edad, y ocupación de la persona con quien tiene una relación. *(Name, age, and occupation of the person with whom you have a relationship.)*_____

1. El rol de la religión y/o la espiritualidad en su vida *(The role of religion and/or spirituality in your life)*:
    A. En la niñez *(During childhood)*_____
    B. En la adultez *(During adulthood)*_____

2. Historial clínico *(Clinical background)*
    A. Describa en sus propias palabras la naturaleza de sus problemas principales y cuanto tiempo han estado presentes. *(Describe in your own words the nature of your main problems and how long you have had them.)*

    _____

    _____

    B. Provea una breve historia del desarrollo de sus problemas desde la primera vez que los experimentó hasta el presente *(Provide a brief history of the development of your problems from the first time that you experienced them to the present time)*:

    _____

    _____

    C. Marque la severidad de sus problemas en la siguiente escala *(Check the severity of your problems on the following scale)*:
        __mínimamente molesto *(mildly upsetting)*
        __moderadamente severo *(moderately severe)*
        __muy severo *(very severe)*
        __extremadamente severo *(extremely severe)*
        __totalmente incapacitante *(totally incapacitating)*

D. ¿Con quién ha usted consultado previamente en relación a su(s) problema(s)? *(Whom have you previously consulted about your problem(s)?)*

_____

_____

E. ¿Está tomando algún medicamento? ¿Cuáles? ¿Qué cantidad tomas? ¿Cuáles han sido los resultados? *(Are you taking any medication? Which ones? How much do you take? What were the results?)*

_____

_____

3. Datos personales *(Personal details)*
   A. Lugar de nacimiento *(Place of birth)* _____
   B. Marque en la lista siguiente aquellos que eran pertinentes a su **niñez** *(check any of the following that were relevant to your **childhood**):*
   __pesadillas *(nightmares)*   __orinarse en la cama *(bedwetting)*
   __caminar dormido *(sleepwalking)* __chuparse el dedo *(thumb sucking)*
   __comerse las uñas *(nail biting)*   __miedos *(fears)*
   __niñez feliz *(happy childhood)*   __niñez infeliz *(unhappy childhood)*
   Algo más no mencionado en la lista *(Anything else not mentioned on the list):*

   _____

   C. Mencione las enfermedades que ha sufrido durante su **niñez**. *(List the illnesses that you had during your **childhood**.)*

   _____

   D. Mencione las enfermedades que ha sufridodurante la **adolescencia**. *(List the illnesses that you had during **adolescence**.)*

   _____

   E. ¿Cuál es su estatura? *(What is your height?)*_____
   ¿Cuál es su peso? *(What is your weight?)*_____
   F. ¿Se ha sometido a operaciones quirúrgicas? *(Have you had any surgical operations?)* Por favor provea una lista de las mismas y la edad cuando fue sometido/a. *(Please provide a list these and the age you were at the time.)*

   _____

   _____

4. Historial sexual *(Sexual background)*
   A. Actitudes de sus padres hacia el sexo. Por ejemplo, ¿habían discusiones familiares o enseñanza en relación al sexo? *(Parental attitudes toward sex. For example, was there any sex education or discussion at home?)*

   _____

   _____

B.   ¿Cuándo y cómo obtuvo usted sus primeros conocimientos en relación a la sexualidad? *(When and how did you first find out about sexuality?)*

_____

_____

C.   Cúando se dió usted cuenta de sus primeros impulsos sexuales? *(When did you first become aware of your own sexual impulses?)*

_____

_____

D.   ¿Ha experimentado algunas ansiedades o sentimientos de culpabilidad originados por el sexo o la masturbación? En caso afirmativo, por favor explique. *(Have you ever experienced any anxieties or feelings of guilt arising from sex or masturbation? If so, please explain.)*

_____

_____

E.   Por favor enumere detalles relevantes en relación a su primera y subsecuentes experiencias sexuales. *(Please list any relevant details regarding your first or subsequent sexual experiences.)*

_____

_____

F.   ¿Es su vida sexual actual satisfactoria? Si no, por favor explique por qué no. *(Is your present sex life satisfactory? If not, please explain why not.)*

_____

_____

G.   Por favor provea información significativa en relación a sus relaciones heterosexuales y/o homosexuales. *(Please provide relevant information with regard to your heterosexual and/or homosexual relations.)*

_____

_____

H.   ¿Se considera usted sexualmente inhibido? *(Would you consider yourself sexually inhibited?)*

_____

_____

5.   Historial familiar *(Family background)*
   A.   Padre *(Father)*
        ¿Aún vive o no? *(Is he still alive or not?)*____
        Si falleció, ¿qué edad tenía usted al momento de su muerte? *(If deceased, how old were you when he died?)*_____
        Causa de su muerte *(Cause of his death)*_____
        Si aún vive, ¿cuál es su edad? *(If he is still alive, how old is he?)*_____
            Su ocupación *(His occupation)*_____
            Su salud *(His health)*_____

Describe la personalidad de su padre y su actitud hacia usted. *(Describe your father's personality and his attitude toward you.)*_____

_____

_____

B.   Madre *(Mother)*

¿Aún vive o no? *(Is she still alive or not?)*_____

Si falleció, ¿qué edad tenía usted al momento de su muerte? *(If deceased, how old were you when she died?)*_____

Causa de su muerte *(Cause of her death)*_____

Si aún vive, ¿cuál es su la edad? *(If she is still alive, how old is she?)*_____

Su ocupación *(Her occupation)*_____

Su salud *(Her health)*_____

Describe la personalidad de su madre y su actitud hacia usted. *(Describe your mother's personality and her attitude toward you.)*_____

_____

C.   Número de hermanos *(Number of brothers)*_____ Edades *(Ages)*_____

Número de hermanas *(Number of sisters)*_____ Edades *(Ages)*_____

D.   Relación con sus hermanos y hermanas *(Relationship with your brothers and sisters)*

Pasado *(Past)*_____

Presente *(Present)*_____

E.   ¿De qué forma fue castigado por sus padres durante su niñez? *(How were you punished by your parents during your childhood?)*

_____

F.   Describa la atmósfera del hogar en donde se crió. *(Describe the atmosphere of the home in which you grew up.)*

_____

G.   ¿Podía compartir cosas íntimas con sus padres? *(Were you able to discuss intimate issues with your parents?)*

6.   Datos personales aditionales *(Additional personal details)*

A.   Describa sus experiencias religiosas o espirituales. *(Describe your religious or spiritual experiences.)*

_____

B.   ¿Quiénes son las personas más importantes en su vida? *(Who are the most important people in your life?)*

_____

    C. Mencione cualquier tipo de experiencia traumática que no haya mencionado anteriormente. *(List any type of traumatic experience that you have not already mentioned.)*

_____

_____

    D. ¿Qué resultados espera obtener de la consejería o terapia? *(What results do you expect from counseling or therapy?)*

_____

_____

    E. Enumere situaciones, objetos, o eventos que le hagan sentirse calmado y relajado. *(List situations, objects, or events that make you feel calm and relaxed.)*

_____

_____

    F. ¿Ha perdido usted el control anteriormente debido al mal humor, llantos, o agresión? En caso afirmativo, descríbalo. *(Have you ever lost control due to bad temper, crying spells or aggression? If so, describe what happened.)*

_____

_____

7. Autodescripción. Por favor complete los siguientes *(Self-description. Please complete the following):*
    A. Yo soy una persona que ... *(I am a person who ...)* _____
    B. Toda mi vida ... *(All my life ...)*_____
    C. Desde que yo era pequeño/a ... *(Since I was little ...)*_____

    D. Una de las cosas por las cuales me siento orgulloso/a es ... *(One of the things that I feel proud of is ...)*_____
    E. Es difícil de admitir que ... *(It is difficult to admit that ...)*_____
    F. Una de las cosas que no puedo perdonar es ... *(One of the things that I cannot forgive is ...)*_____
    G. Una de las cosas por las cuales me siento culpable es ... *(One of the things I feel guilty about is ...)*_____
    H. Mi imagen personal es ... *(My personal image is ...)*_____

    I. Una de las formas en las que otras personas me lastiman es ... *(One of the ways in which other people hurt me is ...)*

_____

    J. Si no tuviera miedo de expresar quien soy yo ... *(If I was not afraid to express who I am ...)*_____

    K. Lo que yo necesito y nunca he recibido de una mujer o un hombre es ... *(What I need and what I have never received from a woman or a man is ...)*_____

8. ¿Qué le gustaría cambiar de su conducta actual? *(What would you like to change about your current behavior?)*

_____

_____

9. ¿Qué sentimientos le gustaría cambiar? *(What feelings would you like to change?)*

_____

_____

10. Describa una imagen placentera de una de sus fantasías. *(Describe a pleasurable image from one of your fantasies.)*

_____

_____

11. Describa:
    A. Su mejor amigo/a. *(Your best friend.)* _____
    B. Alguien a quien usted no le gusta. *(Someone you do not like.)*_____

    _____

12. ¿Usa usted algún tipo de drogas? ¿Cuáles? ¿Desde hace cuánto tiempo? *(Do you use any types of drugs? Which ones? For how long?)*_____

    _____

13. ¿Consume usted alcohol? ¿Cuántas veces al día/semana? *(Do you consume alcohol? How many times a day/week?)*_____

Medical Terms

Identifying Somatic Symptoms

 Cultural hints: Typically, many clients of Latino/Hispanic descent will mask their psychological symptoms with somatic manifestations in order to avoid the implications of a mental health condition, because it is easier to see a physician and "blame" a physical condition than to acknowledge a mental health problem. The following is a list of the body parts that they may point at or that you may refer to when rendering your clinical diagnosis:

Partes del cuerpo	Parts of the body
El abdomen/barriga (coloquial)	Abdomen/belly (colloquial)
El ano	Anus
El antebrazo	Forearm
La boca	Mouth

El brazo	Arm
El cabello	Hair (referring to the head)
La cabeza	Head
La cara	Face
Las cejas	Eyebrows
El codo	Elbow
El cuello	Neck
El cuero cabelludo	Scalp
Los dedos	Fingers
Los dedos de los pies	Toes
Los dientes	Teeth
La espalda	Back
La frente	Forehead
Los hombros	Shoulders
Los labios	Lips
La lengua	Tongue
La mandíbula/la quijada(coloquial)	Jaw
La mano	Hand
Los muslos	Thighs
Las nalgas	Buttocks
La nariz	Nose
El ojo	Eye
El ombligo	Navel/bellybutton
Las orejas	Ears
Las pantorrillas	Calves
El pecho	Chest
El pene	Penis
Las pestañas	Eyelashes
Las piernas	Legs
Los pies	Feet
El pómulo	Cheekbone
El recto	Rectum
Los senos	Breasts
Los testículos	Testicles
Los tobillos	Ankles

Las uñas de las manos	Fingernails
Las uñas de los pies	Toenails
La vagina	Vagina

Vocabulario médico que es parecido en inglés y español	Medical vocabulary that is similar in English and Spanish
Abdomen	Abdomen
Alergia	Allergy
Análisis	Analysis
Antiinflamatorios	Anti-inflammatories
Biopsia	Biopsy
Cáncer	Cancer
Dermatólogo	Dermatologist
Diabetes	Diabetes
Enfisema	Emphysema
Flexible	Flexible
Gastroenterólogo	Gastroenterologist
Genético	Genetic
Hepatitis	Hepatitis
Hereditario	Hereditary
Hipertensión	Hypertension
Imagen	Image
Inflamación	Inflammation
Laringitis	Laryngitis
Maternidad	Maternity
Nutrición	Nutrition
Órganos	Organs
Osteoporosis	Osteoporosis
Penicilina	Penicillin
Proctólogo	Proctologist
Respiratorio	Respiratory
Radiología	Radiology
Rayos-X	X-rays

Sinusitis	Sinusitis
Solución	Solution
Trasplante	Transplant
Tuberculosis	Tuberculosis
Urólogo	Urologist
Vasectomía	Vasectomy
Vómito	Vomit
Xenofobia	Xenophobia

Going to the Emergency Room

It is not a typical for mental health professionals to either escort or refer a client to the emergency room for a mental health evaluation and eventual admittance to a psychiatric unit. Due to some mental health diagnoses that involve physical damage or medical conditions, the counselor must be familiar with this type of vocabulary in order to increase the accuracy of a diagnosis. The following is a list of medical and general terminology that could prove to be useful when deciding if a client should be referred to a clinic or hospital due to self-inflicted wounds, wounds inflicted by another party, or a general medical condition.

La sala de emergencias	The emergency room
El accidente	Accident
La ambulancia	Ambulance
La anestesia	Anesthesia
La caída	(A) fall
El choque de auto	Car crash
La cortadura	Cut
La diabetes	Diabetes
La dislocación	Dislocation
El dolor	Pain
El dolor de pecho	Chest pain
La fractura	Fracture
El golpe	Blow/hit/impact
La herida de bala	Bullet wound
La medicina	Medication

La mordedura	Bite
La navaja	Blade/knife
El oxígeno	Oxygen
El paciente	Patient
La puñalada	Stab wound
Las puntadas	Stitches
El riñón	Kidney
La sala de urgencias	Emergency room
El SIDA	AIDS
El suicidio	Suicide
Las pastillas	Pills
El trauma	Trauma
La víctima	Victim
La violación	Rape
El yeso	Cast
Banda adhesiva	Adhesive band
Alcohol	Alcohol
Vómito	Vomiting
Fiebre	Fever
Gripe	Flu
Dolor de cabeza	Headache
Náusea	Nausea
Palpitaciones	Palpitations
Una erupción	Rash
Dolor de estómago	Stomach ache
Opresión en el pecho	Tightness in the chest
Un resfrío/resfriado	(A) cold
Dificultad para respirar	Breathing difficulty
Calambres	Cramps
Malestar	Discomfort
Vendaje	Bandage
Transfusión de sangre	Blood transfusion
Muletas	Crutches
Gasa	Gauze
Anestesia general	General anesthesia

Anestesia local	Local anesthesia
Agua oxigenada	Hydrogen peroxide
Lesión	Wound/injury
Intoxicación	Intoxication
Hidratación intravenosa	Intravenous hydration
Operación	Operation
Sobredosis	Overdose
Oxígeno	Oxygen
Solución salina	Saline solution
Suero	Serum
Estetoscopio	Stethoscope
Puntos	Stitches
Camilla	Stretcher/hospital bed
Algodón	Swab
Tétano	Tetanus
Antitetánica	Anti-tetanus injection/booster
Vacuna	Vaccine
Signos vitales	Vital signs
Silla de ruedas	Wheelchair

Useful Phrases

The following is a list of phrases that can be useful when inquiring about injuries or medical situations.

Frases prácticas	Practical phrases
¿Cómo se siente?	How do you feel?
¿Dónde está …?	Where is …?
Es …	It is …
¿Está adolorido/a?	Are you in pain?
¿Está embarazada?	Are you pregnant?
¿Está enfermo/a?	Are you sick?
¿Está herido?	Are you hurt?
¿Está mareado/a?	Do you feel dizzy?
¿Está nervioso/a?	Are you nervous?

¿Está quemado/a?	Are you burned?
¿Está tomando medicamentos?	Are you taking medications?
¿Hubo ...?	Was there ...?
¿Hay ...?	Is there/are there ...?
Me siento mal	I feel bad
Me siento bien	I feel fine
¿Qué pasó?	What happened?
¿Llora más de lo normal?	Do you cry more than usual?
¿Ha perdido peso?	Have you lost weight?
¿Tiene ...?	Do you have ...?
¿Se lastimó?	Did you hurt yourself?
¿Quién lo golpeó?	Who hit you?
Respire profundamente	Breathe deeply
¿Se puede mover?	Can you move?
Siéntese, por favor	Sit down, please
No se preocupe	Don't worry
No se mueva	Don't move
Recuéstese en la camilla	Lie down on the stretcher

By removing the question marks, questions that begin with *Está* become statements. Try speaking these phrases with the intonation of a question, and then with the intonation of an affirmative statement. (First listen to both pronunciations.)

¿Tiene calor? (Tiene calor)	Are you hot? (You are hot)
¿Tiene frío? (Tiene frío)	Are you cold? (You are cold)
¿Tiene hambre? (Tiene hambre)	Are you hungry? (You are hungry)
¿Tiene sed? (Tiene sed)	Are you thirsty? (You are thirsty)

Commands

Commands imply action and direction. The following is a list of commands that can assist the counselor in providing immediate help to the client without engaging in long conversations.

Ordenes	Commands
Allá	There
Aquí	Here
Despacio	Slow
Dígame que pasó	Tell me what happened
Escuche	Listen
Mire	Look
Mire aquí	Look here
Míreme	Look at me
Muéstreme	Show me
Muévase aquí	Move here
No se mueva	Don't move
Rápido	Quick
Respire hondo	Breathe deeply
Tome esto	Take this
Vaya	Go

Summary of Previous Concepts with Questions

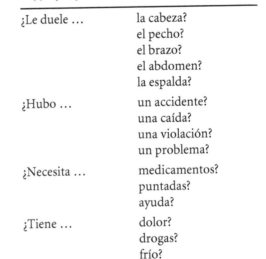

¿Le duele …	la cabeza?
	el pecho?
	el brazo?
	el abdomen?
	la espalda?
¿Hubo …	un accidente?
	una caída?
	una violación?
	un problema?
¿Necesita …	medicamentos?
	puntadas?
	ayuda?
¿Tiene …	dolor?
	drogas?
	frío?
	calor?
	molestias?

¡Traduzca! *(Translate!)*

Have a go at translating the following statements into Spanish. Hint: Read each one out loud first and then listen to the pronunciation on the *reader's companion website*. Make a real effort to look at the previous section for the meaning in each case. Fill the blanks as best you can.

¡Practique!

Frase*(Phrase)*	Traducción*(Translation)*
1. Look at me	
2. Do you need help?	
3. Don't move	
4. Did you hurt yourself?	
5. Did you try to commit suicide?	
6. What is your name?	
7. Are you sick?	
8. Do you have a headache?	

Cultural hints: Some clients may not have US citizenship or residency, and will therefore be somewhat reluctant to visit a clinic facility or office because of their legal status in the country and the potential consequence of deportation. Try to ease the situation by explaining their rights and the obligation of hospital staff to provide them with services regardless of their legal status in the country. Also, make it clear that they will not be reported to the authorities.

Psychological Symptoms

Ruling out or identifying specific conditions or diagnoses based on self-reported symptoms or observations are critical for determining the psychological and emotional status of a client. The following is a list of key words related to psychological symptoms. The list is divided according to the most common diagnoses and their associated symptoms:

Desórdenes de ansiedad (vocabulario general)	Desórdenes de ansiedad (general vocabulary)
Animal	Animal
Ansioso/a	Anxious
Calentura	Fever/high temperature
Corazón golpeando el pecho	Heart pounding in chest

Débil	Weak
Desfallecer	To faint
Dolor de pecho	Chest pain
Escalofríos	Chills
Evento	Event
Evitar	To avoid
Imágenes	Images
Impulso	Impulse
Irritable	Irritable
Lavarse las manos	To wash one's hands
Lugar encerrado/a	Enclosed place
Sentirse mal del estómago	To have stomach ache
Mareado/a	Dizzy
Miedo a morir	Fear of dying
Mucha gente	Many people
Nausea	Nausea
No poder respirar	Shortness of breath/not being able to breathe
Obsesionado/a	Obsessed
Palpitaciones	Palpitations
Pánico	Panic
Perdiendo el control	Losing control
Preocupación constante	Constant worry
Recordar	To remember
Repetir	To repeat
Sangre	Blood
Sensación de ahogo	Feeling of breathlessness/choking
Social	Social
Sudoración	Sweating
Tensión muscular	Muscular tension
Terror	Terror
Trauma	Trauma
Volviéndose loco/a	Going crazy

Esquizofrenia y desordenes psicóticos (vocabulario general)	Schizophrenia and psychotic disorders (general vocabulary)
Actividades diarias	Daily activities
Alucinaciones	Hallucinations
Comunicación incoherente	Incoherent communication
Conducta	Behavior
Confundido/a	Confused
Conversaciones	Conversations
Creencias	Beliefs
Desorganizado/a	Disorganized
Dios	God
Dormir	To sleep
Espíritus	Spirits
Falta de …	Lack of …
Furia	Fury/rage
Influenciado/a	Influenced
Interés	Interest
Llorar	To cry
Moverse	To move (oneself)
Mucho	A lot
Órdenes	Orders
Perplejo	Perplexed
Perseguir	To pursue/chase
Pesadillas	Nightmares
Placer	Pleasure
Poco	A little
Preocupación	Worry/concern
Reírse	To laugh
Sentimientos	Feelings
Sin emoción	Without emotion
Sin movimiento	Motionless
Tiempo	Time
Voces	Voices

Desórdenes de estado de ánimo (vocabulario general)	Mood disorders (general vocabulary)
Actividades	Activities
Apetito	Appetite
Cambios en ...	Changes in ...
Concentrarse	To concentrate
Culpabilidad	Guilt
Energía	Energy
Falta de interés	Lack of interest
Falta de valor	Worthlessness
Insomnio	Insomnia
Muerte	Death
Pensamientos	Thoughts
Peso	Weight
Planes	Plans

El estrés psicosocial (vocabulario general)	Psychosocial stress (general vocabulary)
El abuso	Abuse
La ciudadanía	Citizenship
El divorcio	Divorce
El embarazo	Pregnancy
La enfermedad	Illness
La escuela	School
¿Está asistiendo a la escuela?	Are you attending school?
El idioma	Language
La inmigración	Immigration
Mudarse de la comunidad	To move away from the community
La muerte de un familiar	Death of a relative
Problemas académicos	Academic problems
Las relaciones íntimas	Intimate relationships

La separación	Separation
El empleo	Employment
El desempleo	Unemployment
El trabajo	Work

Desorden de estrés postraumático (vocabulario general)	Post-traumatic stress disorder (general vocabulary)
¿Tiene usted pesadillas?	Do you have nightmares?
¿Qué tipo de pesadillas?	What kind of nightmares?
¿Sólo tiene estas pesadillas mientras duerme o aun estando despierto/a)?	Do you only have these nightmares when you are asleep, or when you are awake as well?
¿Ocurren estas pesadillas frecuentemente?	Do these nightmares occur frequently?
¿Cuán a menudo recuerda estos eventos traumáticos?	How often do you think about these traumatic events?
¿Ha visto algún acto de violencia? ¿Puede describirlo?	Have you witnessed an act of violence? Can you describe it?
¿Ha estado en o visto un accidente de tránsito o de tren?	Have you been in or seen a traffic or train accident?
¿Ha presenciado un huracán, tormenta, terremoto, o erupción de un volcán?	Have you witnessed a hurricane, storm, earthquake, or volcano eruption?
¿Ha estado en una guerra civil?	Have you been in a civil war?
¿Ha sido o visto una violación sexual?	Have you been or seen someone get raped?
¿Ha sido miembro activo del ejército?	Have you been an active member of the army?

Violencia doméstica (vocabulario general)	Domestic violence (general vocabulary)
Abofetear	To slap
Asfixiar	To asphyxiate/suffocate
Estrangular	To strangle/choke

Burlarse	To make fun of
Empujar	To push
Tirar	To throw
Dar/pegar	To hit
Limitar	To limit
Prohibir	To prohibit
Controlar	To control
Encerrar	To lock (in)
Apretar	To hold down/squeeze
Golpear	To batter/beat/thump
Imponerse	To assertoneself
Controlar	To control
Gritar	To yell/shout
Insultar	To insult
Manipular	To manipulate
Ridiculizar	To belittle/ridicule
Patear	To kick
Ignorar	To ignore
Jalar	To pull
Morder	To bite
Destruir	To destroy
Pisar	To step on
Quitar	To take away
Amenazar	To threaten
Vigilar	To watch over or keep an eye on
Sospechar	To suspect
Atacar	To attack
Raspar	To scratch
Ahogar	To suffocate/stifle
La Pareja	Partner
El Miedo	Fear
El Terror	Terror, dread
Intimidar	To intimidate
Enojarse	To get angry
Perder el control	To lose control

Separación	Separation
Divorcio	Divorce
Furia	Anger

Preguntas generales utilizando el vocabulario anterior	**General questions using previous vocabulary**
¿Siente el corazón golpeando el pecho?	Do you feel your heart pounding in your chest?
¿Tiende a lavarse mucho las manos?	Do you tend to wash your hands a lot?
¿Se siente débil?	Do you feel weak?
¿Tiene escalofríos?	Do you have chills?
¿Se siente irritable?	Do you feel irritable?
¿Se siente mal del estómago?	Do you have stomach ache?
¿Siente una sensación de ahogo?	Do you have a feeling of breathlessness/ choking?
¿Siente terror?	Do you feel terrified?
¿Tuvo algún trauma?	Did you have a traumatic experience?
¿Ha perdido el apetito?	Have you lost your appetite?
¿Ha tenido cambios de ánimo?	Have you had mood swings?
¿Tiene insomnio?	Do you have insomnia?
¿Tiene falta de interés por todo?	Do you have a lack of interest in everything?
¿Se divorció?	Did you get divorced?
¿Está embarazada?	Are you pregnant?
¿Hubo muerte de un familiar?	Was there a death in the family?
¿Tiene usted dificultades académicas?	Do you have academic difficulties?
¿Tiene usted relaciones íntimas con su pareja?	Do you have intimate relations with your partner?
¿Tiene usted problemas de inmigración?	Do you have immigration problems?
¿Ha sido abusado/a?	Have you been abused?
¿Cree en Dios?	Do you believe in God?
¿Tiene usted problemas en el trabajo?	Do you have problems at work?
¿Se siente nervioso/a?	Do you feel nervous?

¿Qué le pasa?	What's the matter?
¿Cuántas horas duerme cada noche?	How many hours do you sleep each night?
¿Tiene pensamientos que le preocupan?	Do you have troubling thoughts?

 Cultural hints: Is it psychopathology or a cultural norm? How can you differentiate between appropriate and unusual behaviors? The key points here are the concepts of intensity, duration, and consultation. You have to inquire about the duration of the symptoms and their level of intensity. Are these symptoms disrupting daily activities? Are family and work-related activities affected? It is always a good idea to consult with a native person from the country of origin of the client, if possible, to explore whether or not these symptoms are typical or atypical within the members of that culture and country. If the symptoms and signs are aligned within cultural parameters, then it is up to you to devise a sensitive plan of treatment that addresses the cultural traits of your client.

Lethality Assessment, Suicide Ideation, and Plans

Among the most difficult elements of the therapy process is the proper assessment and evaluation of the emotional and psychological stability of our clients. An incorrect assessment of a client who is experiencing intense emotions or psychological disturbances can have serious implications that could put his or her life at risk. As a result, it is recommended that if your command of the Spanish language is limited, the best course of action is to conduct an assessment only when a more fluent Spanish-speaking colleague or a bilingual interpreter is present. Keep in mind that the safety of our clients must always come first!

Evaluación de Riesgo de Suicidio *(Suicide Risk Evaluation)*

Parte I: Peligro hacia sí mismo/a *(Danger to himself/herself)*

1. **¿Tiene el/la cliente pensamientos suicidas?** *(Does the client have suicidal thoughts?)*
    Sí*(Yes)*__ No*(No)*__

¿Actualmente tiene en mente hacerse daño a sí mismo/a (automutilación o pensamientos suicidas)?	Do you currently think about hurting yourself (self-harm or suicidal thoughts)?
En caso afirmativo, dígame más sobre sus pensamientos.	If so, tell me more about these thoughts.
¿Están estos pensamientos aumentando en frecuencia e/o intensidad?	Are these thoughts increasing in frequency and/or intensity?

¿Se encuentra pensando mucho en torno a estos pensamientos suicidas o solo son pensamientos pasajeros?	Do you find yourself thinking a lot about these suicidal thoughts or are they just fleeting thoughts?
¿Cómo está respondiendo a estos pensamientos? ¿Está pensando demasiado en ellos? ¿Éstos le distraen? ¿Los ignora?	How are you responding to these thoughts? Do you think about them too much? Do they distract you? Do you ignore them?

2. **¿Tiene el/la cliente un plan para suicidarse?** *(Does the client plan to commit suicide?)*
    **Sí*(Yes)* __ No*(No)*__

¿Pasa mucho tiempo planificando como matarse?	Do you spend a lot of time planning how you would kill yourself?
¿Tiene usted un plan específico de como matarse?	Do you have a specific plan for how to kill yourself?
¿Podría ser más específico/a sobre el plan? (i.e. ¿qué, cuándo, dónde, en público, solo/a?)	Can you be more specific about the plan? (i.e. what, when, where, in public, alone?)
¿Tiene usted una fecha para cuando matarse?	Do you have a date for when you plan to kill yourself?
¿Habría algo que pueda evitar que se mate? (i.e. esposo/a, pareja, familia, mascotas, religión, trabajo, amigos/as)	Is there anything that would prevent you from killing yourself? (i.e. spouse, partner, family, pets, religion, work, friends)

3. **¿Tiene el/la cliente facilidad para ejecutar el plan?** *(Is it easy for the client to execute the plan?)*
    **Sí*(Yes)*__ No*(No)*__

¿Cuán accesible es su plan? ¿Tiene usted acceso a un arma de fuego, pastillas, una soga, un edificio alto, veneno, un cuchillo, etc.?	How accessible is your plan? Do you have access to a gun, pills, some rope, a tall building, poison, a knife, etc.?
¿Qué clases de pastillas y cuántas está usted planificando tomar?	What kind of pills and how many are you planning to take?
¿Dónde está el arma de fuego, veneno, u otro objeto letal localizado?	Where is the gun, poison, or other lethal object located?

4.   ¿Tiene el/la cliente un historial de intentos de suicidio? *(Does the client have a history of suicide attempts?)*
Sí*(Yes)__* No*(No)__*

¿Ha intentado suicidarse anteriormente? ¿Cómo? ¿Qué método utilizó? ¿Cuándo fue? ¿Cuántos atentados?¿Estuvo hospitalizado/a? ¿Quién se enteró de la situación?	Have you tried to commit suicide in the past? How? What means did you use? When was it? How many attempts? Where you hospitalized? Who found about it?
¿Intentó usted encubrir este intento de otros/as?	Did you try to hide this attempt from others?
¿Fue el intento accidental o verdaderamente se estaba tratando de matar?	Was the attempt accidental or were you really trying to kill yourself?
¿Ha hecho usted actividades altamente peligrosas? Descríbalas, por favor.	Have you undertaken any highly dangerous activities? Please describe them.
¿Es éste plan suicida diferente a los anteriores?	Is your current suicide plan different from the others in the past?

5.   ¿Tiene el/la cliente alucinaciones y visiones? *(Does the client have hallucinations and visions?)*
Sí*(Yes)__* No*(No)__*

¿Las voces que escucha le están dando órdenes específicas para matarse?	Are the voices you hear giving you specific commands to kill yourself?
¿Tiene usted visiones que le instruyen que se tiene que matar?	Do you have visions that instruct you to kill yourself?
¿Está la radio o la televisión enviando mensajes de que se tiene que matar?	Is the radio or TV sending you messages that you have to kill yourself?
¿Vienen estos mensajes de afuera o del interior de su propia cabeza?	Are these messages coming from outside or inside your own head?
¿Cuán a menudo ésta voz le habla a usted?	How often does this voice talk to you?

¿Cuán a menudo tiene usted éstas visiones?	How often do you have these visions?
¿Qué le dicen las voces?	What are the voices saying?
¿Podría describir las visiones?	Can you describe the visions?
¿Hay algunas otras personas involucradas en las visiones y voces?	Are there any other people involved in the visions and voices?
¿Cómo se siente usted cuando escucha o ve estas visiones? (i.e. asustado/a, consolado/a, adormecido/a, validado/a, etc.)	How do you feel when you hear or see the visions? (i.e. scared, comforted, numbed, validated, etc.)

6. ¿Tiene el/la cliente una red de apoyo y familia? *(Does the client have a support network and family?)*
Sí*(Yes)*__ No*(No)*__

¿Han intentado algunos/as de sus familiares o amigos/as cercanos suicidarse? ¿Lo han logrado?	Have any of your family members or close friends attempted suicide attempts? Did they succeed?
¿Hablan o han hablado estas personas frecuentemente acerca de esto?	Do these people speak or have they spoken about it frequently?
¿Cómo le impactó los intentos de suicidios de estos/as?	What impact did their suicide attempts have on you?
¿Se sintió usted inspirado/a o decepcionado por ellos?	Did you feel inspired by them or disappointed in them?

Parte II: Peligro para los demás *(Danger to others)*

1. ¿Tiene el/la cliente pensamientos homicidas? *(Does the client have homicidal thoughts?)*
Sí*(Yes)*__ No*(No)*__

¿Tiene usted pensamientos frecuentes en torno a lastimar o matar a alguien?	Do you have frequent thoughts of hurting or killing anyone?
Describa estos pensamientos. Por favor provea los detalles.	Describe these thoughts. Please provide details.
¿Son estos pensamientos sobre alguien en específico? ¿Quién?	Are these thoughts about someone in particular? Who?

¿Está esta persona cerca o lejos de usted?	Is this person near or far away from you?
¿Cuánto le tomaría a usted hallar a esta persona?	How long would it take you to find this person?
¿Cuán a menudo piensa usted en hacerle daño a esta persona?	How often do you think about hurting this person?
¿Se ha imaginado a usted mismo/a ejecutando este plan en contra de esta persona?	Have you imagined yourself carrying out this plan against this person?
¿Cuán intensos son estos pensamientos? ¿Continúan aumentando o han disminuido?	How intense are these thoughts? Do they keep growing or have they diminished?

2.   **¿Tiene el/la cliente pensamientos violentos y un plan de acción para cometer violencia?** (*Does the client have violent thoughts and an action plan to commit violence?*)
     Sí(*Yes*)__ No(*No*)__

¿Quién está involucrada en su plan? ¿Está pensando involucrar a otros/as para llevar a cabo su plan?	Who is involved in your plan? Are you planning to involve anyone else to help you carry out this plan?
¿Qué fecha tiene propuesta para llevar a cabo su plan?	What date do you propose to carry out the plan?
¿Qué herramientas necesita para llevar a cabo este plan? (i.e. armas, medicamentos, etc.)	What tools do you need to carry out the plan? (i.e. weapons, medication, etc.)
¿Se siente seguro/a de su plan?	Do you feel confident about your plan?

3.   **¿Tiene el/la cliente un historial de violencia?** (*Does the client have a history of violence?*)
     Sí(*Yes*)__ No(*No*)__

Ha cometido actos violentos contra otros/as? ¿Cuándo? ¿Contra quién?	Have you committed violent acts toward others? When? Against whom?

¿Se arrepiente usted de sus acciones pasadas? Do you regret your past actions?

¿Ha sido usted víctima de violencia o abuso por parte de otros/as? Have you been a victim of violence or abuse by others?

¿Ha tenido usted cargos en su contra o ha sido convicto/a por agresión en el pasado? Have you ever been charged or convicted of assault in the past?

Evaluación general y final *(General and final evaluation)*

Presentación y aspecto del cliente. Conteste sí o no a las siguientes. *(Presentation and appearance of the client. Answer yes or no to the following.)*

Agitado/a	Sí__No__	Agitated	Yes__ No__
Ansioso/a	Sí__ No__	Anxious	Yes__ No__
Bajo la influencia de drogas o alcohol	Sí__ No__	Under the influence of drugs or alcohol	Yes__ No__
Cambios de ánimo (ej. de contento/a a triste a furioso/a)	Sí__ No__	Changes in mood (e.g. f romhappy to sad to angry)	Yes__ No__
Cambios de apetito	Sí__ No__	Changes in appetite	Yes__ No__
Delirante	Sí__ No__	Delerious	Yes__ No__
Deprimido/a	Sí__ No__	Depressed	Yes__ No__
Desorientado/a	Sí__ No__	Disoriented	Yes__ No__
Distante	Sí__ No__	Aloof	Yes__ No__
Furioso/a	Sí__ No__	Angry	Yes__ No__
Hostil	Sí__ No__	Hostile	Yes__ No__
Incoherente	Sí__ No__	Incoherent	Yes__ No__
Indefenso/a	Sí__ No__	Helpless	Yes__ No__
Indiferente	Sí__ No__	Indifferent	Yes__ No__
Paranoide	Sí__ No__	Paranoid	Yes__ No__
Preocupado/a	Sí__ No__	Preoccupied	Yes__ No__
Tenso/a	Sí__ No__	Tense	Yes__ No__
Triste	Sí__ No__	Sad	Yes__ No__

Puntaje final *(Final score)*

Add the numbers of affirmative answers. Determine what course of action should be taken.

Parte I: Peligro hacia sí mismo/a *(Danger to himself/herself)*

1. ¿Tiene el/la cliente pensamientos suicidas? *(Does the client have suicidal thoughts?)*

   Sí*(Yes)__* No*(No)__*

2. ¿Tiene el/lacliente tiene un plan para suicidarse? *(Does the client plan to commit suicide?)*
   Sí *(Yes)__* No*(No)__*

3. ¿Tiene el/lacliente tiene facilidad para ejecutar el plan? *(Is it easy for the client to execute the plan?)*
   Sí *(Yes) __* No*(No)__*

4. ¿Tiene el/la cliente un historial de intentos de suicidio? *(Does the client have a history of suicide attempts?)*
   Sí *(Yes)__* No*(No)__*

5. ¿Tiene el/la cliente alucinaciones y visiones? *(Does the client have hallucinations and visions?)*
   Sí *(Yes)__* No*(No)__*

6. ¿Tiene el/la cliente una red de apoyo y familia? *(Does the client have a support network and family?)*
   Sí *(Yes) __* No*(No)__*

Parte II: Peligro para los demás*(Danger to others)*

1. ¿Tiene el/la cliente pensamientos homicidas? *(Does the client have homicidal thoughts?)*
   Sí *(Yes)__* No*(No)__*

2. ¿Tiene el/la cliente pensamientos violentos y un plan de acción para cometer violencia? *(Does the client have violent thoughts and an action plan to commit violence?)*
   Sí *(Yes)__* No*(No)__*

3. ¿Tiene el/la cliente un historial de violencia? *(Does the client have a history of violence?)*
   Sí *(Yes)__* No*(No)__*

Resumen de Evaluación de Riesgo de Suicidio *(Summary of Suicide Risk Assessment)*

	Ninguno *(None)*	Bajo *(Low)*	Moderado *(Moderate)*	Alto *(High)*
Peligro hacia sí mismo/a *(Danger to himself/herself)*				
Peligro para los demás *(Danger to others)*				
Commentarios *(Comments)*				

¿El/la cliente desea ayuda? *(Does the client want help?)* Sí (Yes) ___ No *(No)*___

¿El/la cliente vino en contra de su voluntad para solicitar ayuda? *(Did the client come against his/her own will to get help?)* Sí (Yes) ___ No *(No)*___

Crisis Intervention Treatment Plan and Cultural Considerations

Since the main goal of a crisis intervention is to bring the client back to the pre-crisis or normalcy stage, it is above all instrumental to ensure the personal safety and well-being of the client. Make sure that your client is not under the influence of alcohol or any other drug that could taint the entire evaluation process. Whether or not the client is behaving erratically because of the influence of substances, our main responsibility is to protect the client.

 Cultural hints: Since many Latino/Hispanic clients hold deep spiritual connections, we must exercise caution when evaluating the concept of voices and commands. It is not atypical for individuals to have dreams, visions, or hear voices in which a command has been given. This could be construed as a normal cultural reaction *if* none of these commands are based on harming themselves or hurting others. If the visions are based on personal growth, helping someone, not getting a haircut, avoiding certain types of foods, liquor, tobacco, or doing certain activities, then it is not harming the client or anyone else. Then again, if these activities are affecting normal daily activities, friends, and family relationships, then there is a psychopathology aspect that must be explored. To make sure that your assessment is accurate, (especially when in doubt) always consult a native Latino/Hispanic individual who is in tune with the same culture as your client.

Algunas medicinas y remedios caseros relacionados con enfermedades emocionales	Some medicines and home remedies related to emotional illnesses
Té de manzanilla	Chamomile tea
Té (mate)	Tea
Hierbas	Herbs
Tranquilizante	Tranquilizer
Antidepresivos	Antidepressants
Pastillas/píldoras/tabletas	Pills
Calmantes	Sedatives
Jarabe	Syrup
Hipnóticos	Hypnotics

Inyección	Injection
Acetaminofen	Acetaminophen
Anti-alérgeno	Anti-allergen
Aspirina	Aspirin
Antiácido	Antacid
Antihistamínico	Antihistamine
Cortisona	Cortisone
Morfina	Morphine
Insulina	Insulin
Codeína	Codeine

Case Study 4: Ana María

Background: Ana María is a devout Catholic woman from Guatemala who has a mixed Spanish–Indigenous background. She is 41 years old and has limited formal education (5th grade elementary school level). Ana María is a recent immigrant who works picking fruit in the strawberry fields, has five children, and a husband with a history of domestic violence and alcoholism. She came accompanied by her neighbor to the community agency where you work, which provides services to recent Latino/Hispanic immigrants. Her neighbor said that she was worried because Ana María seemed to be "possessed by a spirit or something." She has been crying non-stop since her miscarriage a couple of days ago. (*Ana María es una mujer muy católica de Guatemala de mestizaje español e indígena. Ella tiene 41 años de edad y una educación formal limitada (a nivel de 5to grado de escuela elemental). Ana María es una inmigrante reciente que trabaja recogiendo fruta en los campos de fresas, tiene cinco niños y un marido con una historia de violencia y alcoholismo. Ella vino acompañada de su vecina a la agencia comunitaria donde usted trabaja, la cual provee servicios a inmigrantes recientes latinos/hispanos. La vecina de ésta estaba preocupada porque parecía ser que Ana María estaba "poseída por un espíritu o algo así." Ella ha estado llorando sin cesar desde que tuvo un aborto espontáneo hace dos días.*)

Consejera: Buenas tardes Ana María. Mi nombre es la Sra. Thomas y trabajo como consejera de salud mental en la agencia. Parece ser que estás pasando por un momento difícil. ¿Me podría decir que le está sucediendo? (*Good afternoon Ana María. My name is Ms. Thomas and I work as a counselor at the mental health agency. It seems that you are going through a difficult time. Can you tell me what is happening to you?*)

Ana María:	Perdone la molestia. Yo no debería estar aquí sino en mi casa atendiendo a mis hijos. *(I apologize for the trouble. I shouldn't be here, but should be at home taking care of my children.)*
Consejera:	Parece ser que amas mucho a sus hijos y se preocupa por su bienestar. *(It seems that you love your children and are concerned about their well-being.)*
Ana María:	Sí, ellos son todo para mí. Por eso me duele que perdí a … *(Yes, they are everything to me. That's why it hurts me that I lost …)*
Consejera:	¿Perdió a su bebé? *(Did you lose your baby?)*
Ana María:	Yo creo que fue castigo de Dios. Estoy casi segura que fue eso. Quizás la Virgen … *(I believe that it was God's punishment. I am almost sure that it was that. Perhaps the Virgin …)*
Consejera:	Antes que nada, lo siento mucho, no debe haber sido nada fácil. ¿Usted mencionó la Virgen? ¿Qué pasó? Continúe, por favor. *(First and foremost, I am very sorry, it must not have been easy at all. You mentioned the Virgin? Please continue.)*
Ana María:	Usted va a pensar que yo estoy loca. *(You are going to think that I am crazy.)*
Consejera:	Estás en un lugar donde puedes hablar con confianza y sentirte que no vas a ser juzgada. *(You are in place where you can speak freely and feel that you will not be judged.)*
Ana María:	Hace un tiempo que le había prometido a la Virgen Santa María de Suyapa que si le daba salud a Carlitos, mi hijo menor, entonces le iba a enviar una donación a la iglesia allá en la comunidad. Con el tiempo, se me olvidó, y por eso fue que perdí a mi último bebé. *(A while ago I promised the Virgin Saint Mary of Suyapa that if she granted health to Carlitos, my youngest son, then I would send a donation to the church over there in the community. With time, I forgot, and that is why I lost my last baby.)*
Consejera:	Debe ser muy difícil por lo que está pasando. Lo siento mucho. *(It must be very difficult what you are going through. I am very sorry.)*
Ana María:	Así vienen los castigos divinos. Anoche oí una voz que me dijo que tenía que peregrinar allá en el verano para llevarle ofrenda. *(This is how divine punishments are delivered. Last night I heard a voice that told me that I must make a pilgrimage over to the church in the summer to take the donation.)*
Consejera:	¿Y qué más le dijo la Virgen? *(And what else did the Virgin tell you?)*
Ana María:	Me dio algunas instrucciones que tengo que seguir. *(She gave me some instructions that I must follow.)*
Consejera:	¿Podría decirme algunas de esas instrucciones? *(Can you tell me some of these instructions?)*

Ana María: Son muy personales. *(They are very personal.)*

Consejera: Yo entiendo. Pero ¿me podría decir si la Virgen le dio órdenes de hacerse daño a sí misma, a sus hijos, o a su marido? *(I understand. But could you tell me if the Virgin gave you orders to hurt yourself, your children, or your husband?)*

Ana María: ¡No, no! Eso lo hubiera dicho el diablo. Es que me siento muy vacía por dentro por haber abandonado la virgencita y haber olvidado las promesas que le había hecho. *(No, no! That would have been said by the devil. It is just that I feel very empty inside for having abandoned the Virgin and for having forgotten the promises that I had made to her.)*

Consejera: Vamos a hacer una cosa. Yo le voy a hacer unas preguntas y si usted me las contesta, entonces yo voy a poder brindarle mucho mejor ayuda. ¿Sí? *(Let's do something. I am going to ask you some questions and if you answer them, then I will be able to provide you with better assistance.)*

Ana María: De acuerdo. *(All right.)*

Consejera: ¿Ha pensado hacerse daño por medio de pastillas, un arma, o algo así? *(Have you thought of harming yourself by using pills, a weapon, or something like that?)*

Ana María: ¡No, no! Ya se lo había dicho. *(No, no! I already told you.)*

Consejera: Sí, lo entiendo, pero es que tengo que estar segura. ¿Y ha pensado hacerle daño a su esposo? *(Yes, I understand, but I have to be sure. And have you thought of harming your husband?)*

Ana María: Aunque ya no lo quiero, todavía lo respeto y no me atrevería hacerle nada. Además, nosotros los católicos no hacemos eso. Eso sería lo peor que le podría hacer a mi virgencita. *(Even though I don't love him anymore, I still respect him and I would not dare to do anything to him. Anyway, we Catholics do not do not that. That would be the worst thing that I could do to my Virgin.)*

Consejera: ¿Ha estado consumiendo mucho alcohol durante estas últimas semanas? *(Have you been consuming a lot of alcohol during the last few weeks?)*

Ana María: Yo ni bebo ni fumo. *(I neither drink nor smoke.)*

Consejera: ¿Piensa en morirse de vez en cuando? *(Do you think about dying once in a while?)*

Ana María: No, no puedo abandonar a mis hijos. ¿Quién los cuidaría si yo no estoy? Su papá siempre está trabajando y cuando está en casa, siempre está borracho. *(No, I cannot abandon my children. Who would take care of them if I were not here? Their dad is always working and when he is at home, he is always drunk.)*

Consejera: ¿A usted le molestaría si en algún momento incluimos en esta conversación al sacerdote de la parroquia local? *(Would you mind if at some point we bring the priest from the local parish into this conversation?)*

Ana María: No, para nada. A lo mejor él me puede decir que hacer con lo de las instrucciones que me dio la virgencita. *(No, not at all. He could probably tell me what to do about the instructions that the Virgin gave me.)*

Consejera: Perfecto. Claro que sí. *(Perfect. Of course.)*

Ana María: ¿Me van a meter al hospital? *(Are they going to put me in hospital?)*

Consejera: No, no. Quizás se quede aquí un rato más para que entonces se vaya por la tarde. Solo queremos estar seguros que usted va a estar bien al igual que sus hijos. *(No, no. Maybe you will have to stay here for a little while before you leave later in the afternoon. We just want to make sure that both you and your children will be all right.)*

Ana María: Gracias, gracias. ¿Cómo le puedo pagar? *(Thank you, thank you. How can I pay you?)*

Consejera: De nada. La parte económica la puede discutir con la secretaria administrativa en el mostrador. Lo que necesito es que se comprometa conmigo que va a poner de su parte y va a venir a la siguiente sesión cuando el sacerdote de la parroquia este aquí. *(You're welcome. The billing arrangements can be discussed with the administrative secretary at the registration desk. What I need from you is a promise of your commitment to come to the next session when the priest of the parish will be here.)*

Ana María: ¡Absolutamente! *(Absolutely!)*

Case Study 5: Juan Manuel

Juan Manuel works for a meat packing company as a butcher. He does the night shifts (12.00am–7.00am) and was referred to you (a human resources psychologist) by his supervisor due to his erratic behavior at work. Juan Manuel has had multiple episodes of marked hostility against co-workers and two episodes of insubordination against supervisors. He has had four warnings and his job status depends upon the outcome of this interview with you. *(Juan Manuel trabaja para una procesadora de carne como carnicero. Él trabaja el turno de la madrugada (12:00am–7:00am) y fue referido a usted (un psicólogo de recursos humanos) por su supervisor debido a su conducta errática en el trabajo. Juan Manuel ha tenido varios episodios de violencia en contra de algunos de sus compañeros de trabajo y dos episodios de insubordinación en contra de sus supervisores. Él ha tenido cuatro advertencias y el estatus de su trabajo depende del resultado de esta entrevista con usted.)*

Psicólogo:	Buenos días, Sr. Juan Manuel. ¿Cómo está? (*Good morning, Mr. Juan Manuel. How are you?*)
Juan Manuel:	Hola, no estoy bien. Creo que me van a despedir del trabajo. (*Hello, I am not well. I think that they are going to fire me.*)
Psicólogo:	Por favor, dígame qué ha pasado. (*Please, tell what has happened.*)
Juan Manuel:	Es que me he estado peleando con mis compañeros y mis jefes. (*The thing is, I have been arguing with my co-workers and bosses.*)
Psicólogo:	Hábleme sobre eso. ¿Qué pasó en específico? (*Tell me about that. What exactly happened?*)
Juan Manuel:	Estoy confundido, tengo mucha rabia adentro. A veces me siento que quisiera … (*I am confused, I have a lot of anger inside. Sometimes I feel like I would like to …*)
Psicólogo:	¿Sí? Continúe, por favor … (*Yes? Please continue …*)
Juan Manuel:	Creo que nada vale la pena en esta vida. Nada. (*I believe that nothing is worth doing in this life. Nothing.*)
Psicólogo:	¿Nada en lo absoluto? (*Absolutely nothing?*)
Juan Manuel:	Lo que pasa es que uno trabaja mucho para nada, nada. Es que uno se mata trabajando y por más que trabaja todo le sale mal. La vida apesta. (*What happens is that one works a lot for nothing, nothing. The thing is that one kills oneself working and no matter how hard one works, everything goes wrong. Life stinks.*)
Psicólogo:	"Nada" y "todo" son palabras bien generales. (*"Nothing" and "everything" are very general words.*)
Juan Manuel:	No sé si vale la pena vivir para recibir insultos … (*I don't know if it is worth living to receive insults …*)
Psicólogo:	O sea, que usted quisiera estar muerto, ¿es así? (*So, you would like to be dead, is that right?*)
Juan Manuel:	Muchas veces … sí. (*Quite often … yes.*)
Psicólogo:	O sea, que ¿usted quisiera matarse o hacerse daño? (*So, you would like to kill or harm yourself?*)
Juan Manuel:	Más o menos. A veces me pasa por la cabeza. (*More or less. Sometimes it crosses my mind.*)
Psicólogo:	¿Cuán a menudo? (*How often?*)
Juan Manuel:	Unas cuantas veces a la semana. (*A few times a week.*)
Psicólogo:	¿Cuántas veces específicamente? (*How many times exactly?*)
Juan Manuel:	No sé, tres o cuatro veces. Más o menos. (*I don't know, three or four times. More or less.*)
Psicólogo:	¿Y tiene un plan de cómo matarse? (*And do you have a plan for how to kill yourself?*)
Juan Manuel:	Bueno … tengo un rifle en el sótano de la casa y una bala

	específica para eso. *(Well ... I have a rifle in the basement of the house and a bullet specifically for it.)*
Psicólogo:	¿Cuándo lo piensa hacer? *(When are you planning on doing it?)*
Juan Manuel:	En la noche, cuando todos duermen. *(At night, when everyone is asleep.)*
Psicólogo:	¿Alguien más lo sabe? *(Does anyone else know about it?)*
Juan Manuel:	Yo se lo he comentado a mi esposa pero ella no me hace caso. *(I have mentioned it to my wife but she doesn't pay any attention to me.)*
Psicólogo:	¿Usted cree que su esposa e hijos le aman? *(Do you believe that your wife and children love you?)*
Juan Manuel:	Sí. *(Yes.)*
Psicólogo:	¿Cree que le van a extrañar si usted les falta? *(Do you think that they will miss you if you are not there?)*
Juan Manuel:	Bueno ... creo que sí. *(Well ... I think so.)*
Psicólogo:	Sé que ha tenido problemas con varias personas en el trabajo. ¿Ha pensado hacerle daño a alguien? *(I know that you have had problems with some people at work. Have you thought of harming anyone?)*
Juan Manuel:	No, no. Bien, me gustaría darle una cachetada al supervisor, pero eso es todo. Yo no le haría daño a nadie. *(No, no. Well, I would like to slap my supervisor in the face, but that's all. I would not harm anyone.)*
Psicólogo:	¿Cuánto alcohol consume a la semana? *(How much alcohol do you consume each week?)*
Juan Manuel:	Unas cervezas cada noche luego que salgo del trabajo. *(Some beers every night after work.)*
Psicólogo:	¿Cuántas? *(How many?)*
Juan Manuel:	No sé, no las cuento. Pero mi esposa me dice que soy un borracho. Creo que exagera. *(I don't know, I don't count them. But my wife says that I am a drunk. I think she exaggerates.)*
Psicólogo:	O sea, que todos los días consume alcohol. ¿Y siempre se emborracha? *(So, you consume alcohol every day. And do you always get drunk?)*
Juan Manuel:	No, no siempre. Cuatro o cinco veces a la semana. Eso es normal. *(No, not always. Four or five times a week. That's normal.)*
Psicólogo:	¿Cuán importante es la religión para usted? *(How important is religion to you?)*
Juan Manuel:	Siempre voy los domingos a misa y escucho al sacerdote. *(I always go to mass on Sundays and listen to the priest.)*
Psicólogo:	O sea, que ¿usted tiene una creencia firme en Dios? *(So, you have a firm belief in God?)*

Juan Manuel:	Soy católico. *(I am Catholic.)*
Psicólogo:	¿Cómo usted cree que el sacerdote se sentiría al saber que usted se suicidó? *(How do you think that the priest will feel when he finds out that you committed suicide?)*
Juan Manuel:	Muy mal, triste, decepcionado. Y Dios también. *(Very bad, sad, disappointed. And God too.)*
Psicólogo:	¿Todavía se quiere matar? *(Do you still want to kill yourself?)*
Juan Manuel:	Es que me siento atrapado, sin opciones y triste … la vida … *(It is just that I feel trapped, without options and sad … life …)*
Psicólogo:	Juan Manuel, como parte de mi trabajo, mi función es proteger la vida de mis clientes y ahora mismo usted necesita mucha ayuda, la cual yo no puedo brindar. Sin embargo, hay profesionales que le brindarán ayuda inmediata y le darán apoyo para superar su crisis. Es necesario que esté en el hospital unos días por su bien. *(Juan Manuel, as part of my work, my job is to protect the lives of my clients and right now you need a lot of help, help that I cannot provide. However, there are professionals who will provide immediate assistance and will give you support to surpass your crisis. For your own good, it is necessary that you go to hospital for a few days.*
Juan Manuel:	¿Me está diciendo que estoy loco? *(Are you saying that I am crazy?)*
Psicólogo:	No, en lo absoluto. Solo digo que necesita un poco de ayuda adicional, eso es todo. *(Absolutely not. I am only saying that you need some additional help, that's all.)*
Juan Manuel:	¿Pero qué va a pasar con mi trabajo? ¿Me van a despedir? ¿Y mi familia? *(But what's going to happen with my job? Are they going to fire me? And my family?)*
Psicólogo:	Todo es confidencial y nadie va a saber por qué está en el hospital. Su trabajo no lo puede perder por esta situación. No se preocupe. *(Everything is confidential and nobody will know why you are in hospital. You cannot lose your job because of this situation. Don't worry.)*
Juan Manuel:	¿Está seguro que todo va a salir bien? *(Are you sure that everything will turn out well?)*
Psicólogo:	Mi compromiso es facilitarle toda la ayuda posible y vamos a estar trabajando muy de cerca con sus empleadores. *(My commitment is to give you all the possible help you can get and we will be working closely with your employer.)*
Juan Manuel:	Gracias … *(Thank you …)*

5 Interventions for School Counselors and School Psychologists

A Quick Overview of the School Counseling Culture

The school environment is vastly different from the mental health arena (e.g., community counseling, substance abuse, and vocational counseling) because school counselors operate within an educational environment led by a teaching philosophy enforced by teachers and school administrators. In most cases, school counselors started out in teaching before moving into the discipline of school counseling. As a result, most school counselors know how to navigate the educational system and maintain productive relationships with teachers and administrators. School counselors are aware that psychological and behavioral interventions are designed to expedite the academic progress of the students. This section is intended to provide a quick overview for counselors who may have worked mostly in mental health settings but are transitioning into the school counseling discipline, and also for school counselors who have had minimal contact with bilingual populations but are either facing an influx of Spanish speakers in their schools, or have perhaps recently moved to a new school district. Many states have now allowed mental health practitioners to be eligible to practice as school counselors by relaxing long-standing traditional requirements for teaching experience and licensure (Baker & Gerler, Jr., 2008). In this way, many schools have filled their shortages of school counselors resulting from a wave of retirees. Consequently, many mental health counselors have obtained the necessary college credits to compensate for a lack of pedagogical expertise in order to become certified school counselors. Regardless of whether or not school counselors come from a teaching or a mental health background, the lack of linguistic and cultural tools for dealing with a large number of monolingual Spanish-speaking students is equally challenging for both.

Bilingual Populations

In compliance with the Comprehensive School Guidance model sponsored by the American School Counseling Association (ASCA), school counselors promote a developmental K–12 approach to counseling. The emphasis is to promote growth by targeting students' personal and social issues, their career, and their academic development (Yuen, Lau & Chan, 2000). Unlike the mental health paradigm, whose objective is to bring the individual back to the pre-crisis or normalcy stage by means of psychological and behavioral interventions, the emphasis of the school counselor's interventions is to assist the student to cope with day-to-day issues and concerns in order to promote academic success (American Counseling Association, 2005).

With this framework in mind, if you ask most people what they know about bilingual programs or bilingual students in our schools, the majority – even teachers in the field – will associate these with so-called minority or ethnically underrepresented populations and ESL (English as a Second Language) or LEP (Limited English Proficiency) programs. In spite of the fact that we live in the most ethnically, racially, and linguistically diverse country on earth, the educational system and the media have associated a "handicapped" image with the acquisition of languages. In other words, those who speak more than one language are associated with immigrant or undocumented populations who consequently have academic deficiencies. This paradigm is entrenched by the promotion of a monocultural and monolingual society, which is intented to sustain uniformity. In contrast, multilingualism is the norm on most continents such as Europe, Africa, and Asia. Of course, this does not preclude the fact that these multilingual and multicultural dynamics are challenging, as reflected in all the political and social turmoil that it may produce. However, multilingualism and multiculturalism are realities that cannot be put aside by ignoring them or by creating different statuses and laws that promote forced monolingualism; people will neither learn English overnight nor forget their native tongue following the stroke of a pen.

In essence, bilingual education in the US is defined as the use of English and another language for instructional objectives (Castro-Feinberg, 2002). According to Krashen (1996), this type of bilingual education should encompass instruction in English at school with a combination of literacy instruction and reinforcement of content areas provided through the home language.

Since this book is devoted to Spanish-speaking populations, I will emphasize the current situation of Spanish–English bilingual students, specifically those who are native Spanish speakers. If you are in a school that does not have a considerable amount of Spanish-speaking immigrants, it is likely that there is no formal ESL or bilingual program being implemented. Perhaps the school operates under the *submersion* philosophy, namely, the sink-or-swim model (Hakuta, Butler & Witt, 2000). In other words, the non-English-speaking students are expected to learn English by forced immersion without bilingual assistance. To bring this into perspective, imagine that as an adolescent or young child you immigrate to Germany with your parents and are placed in their school system with no previous knowledge of the language or culture. Of course, you are expected to adjust, do well and perhaps even excel within a year! It is not going to be the most pleasurable experience.

As mentioned in Chapter One, Spanish-speaking students come from diverse backgrounds (i.e., racial, economic, educational, political, and geographical), but by and large they share a series of variables that put them in a disadvantaged position. Some of these variables are as follows:

(a) their parents are likely to have a level of education lower than that of high school or its equivalent,

(b) their household income is below the US average and many live on the threshold of poverty,

(c) over 80 percent or more qualify for free or reduced cost lunch at school,

(d) a vast majority came to the US with a limited or poor academic background from their home countries,

(e) many live in high-crime neighborhoods,

(f) Spanish is mostly spoken at home, and parents are consequently unable to assist with most school work, which involves the English language,

(g) the pursuit of a higher education degree is not a value instilled at home due to their immediate economic needs,

(h) they struggle against racial and ethnic stigmatization in a new cultural environment, and

(i) they have a lack of knowledge of US culture, norms, and social conventions (Rodríguez-Pino, 1997; Thomas & Collier, 1997; Valdés, 2000).

The Myth of Bilingualism in the US: The Influx of Latinos/Hispanics

There is a prevalent myth that bilingual education and the struggles that schools face in assisting new immigrants constitutes a new phenomenon in the US. It is important to realize that there have been many waves of immigrants in the US and the Latino/Hispanic wave is just the latest one. In fact, our nation has been facing linguistic challenges since the 1500s during the Spanish conquest and pre-British colonization. For example, in 1738, close to St. Augustine, Florida, which was the first permanent European settlement in the continental US, a community of free Africans was established with the authorization of the Spanish government on the condition that they relinquish their native tongues (i.e. Guineans, Minas, Araras, Sambas, Mandingos, Congos), convert to Catholicism, and speak Spanish (Johnson & Smith, 1999). This is just one of many examples throughout the history of the US of widespread changes in attitude towards bilingualism and monolingualism. It is therefore easy to realize that bilingualism in the US is not a new social, educational, or political issue. It is expected that the inception of a new nation of immigrants will provoke issues related to culture and language collisions. As a result, we are constantly amending how we conduct business, by changing our policies and adjusting our professional standards in order to provide services more efficiently. These signs of struggles and changes are positive ones, which show that we are willing to adapt as a nation and as a group of professionals.

Learning and Teaching Styles

Latino/Hispanic children are taught to respect and honor their family. Classroom competition among students may bring much discomfort to Latino/Hispanic families, as their culture focuses largely on working together whereas the

U.S. educational system is primarily focused on individual achievement and performance. The emphasis on cooperation and group achievement at times takes precedence over the specific performance of just one person. It is critical for school counselors and psychologists to be aware of Latino/Hispanic students' level of English, as behavioral issues and poor academic performance may be related to their inability to express themselves properly using the English language. The student may need additional language support or an assistant Spanish-speaking teacher.

School Terminology and Concepts

Now, let's get to work on your school counseling vocabulary. This table provides general terminology of events, objects, or people associated with school settings and school counseling tasks. Some terms, concepts, or words have been purposefully omitted in this section because they have been covered in previous chapters. So it is a matter of integrating the words that you learned before and placing them in a school context; for example, the parts of the body and greetings apply to any school counseling or mental health setting.

Vocabulario escolar general	General school vocabulary
El asiento	Seat
El bolígrafo	Pen
El/la consejero/a	Counselor
El/la consejero/a académico/a	School counselor
El cuaderno	Notebook
El/laprincipal	Principal
La escuela	School
El/la estudiante	Student
El lápiz	Pencil
El libro	Book
El/la maestro/a	Teacher
El salón	Classroom
La tarea	Homework
El uniforme	Uniform
Los zapatos	Shoes

The following tables provide vocabulary related to these three domains in terms of our work with children, adolescents, and their relatives. The vocabulary and concepts are especially relevant to school settings.

Área de las cogniciones/pensamientos (Cognitive/Thoughts Domain)

The cognitive (thoughts) domain consists of areas that place primary emphasis on the mental or intellectual processes of the student (client). These processes are: synthesis, evaluation, knowledge, application, comprehension, and analysis (Papalia, Wendkos, Duskin & Feldman, 2004). These areas are normally reflected in the behavior of the student.

Área de las cogniciones/pensamientos (vocabulario general)	Cognitive/thoughts domain (general vocabulary)
Abstracto/a	Abstract
Acordarse	To remember
Alerta	Alert
Analfabeto/a	Illiterate
Análisis	Analysis
Aplicación	Application
Brillante	Brilliant
Buenos pensamientos	Good thoughts
Comprensión	Understanding
Concreto/a	Concrete
Conocimiento	Knowledge
Creativo/a	Creative
Curioso/a	Curious
Deficiencia intelectual	Intellectual deficiency
Diestro/a	Skilled
Discapacidad mental	Mental disability
Distraído/a	Distracted
Entender	To understand/grasp
Evaluación	Evaluation
Fantasía	Fantasy
Habilidad	Ability

Área de las cogniciones/pensamientos (vocabulario general)	Cognitive/thoughts domain (general vocabulary)
La idea	Idea
La imaginación	Imagination
Instruido	Instructed
Inteligencia	Intelligence
Malos pensamientos	Bad thoughts
Normal	Normal
Olvidadizo/a	Forgetful/absent minded
Olvidarse	To forget
Retardación mental	Mental retardation
Talentoso/a	Talented/gifted

Área afectiva/emocional (Affective/Emotional Domain)

The affective (emotional) domain consists of areas that place primary emphasis on the values, emotions, and attitudes of the student (client), which are normally reflected by adjustments, appreciations, and interests (Papalia, Wendkos, Duskin & Feldman, 2004). The affective domain, especially when working with children and adolescents, is more vague than the cognitive domain. However, it is perhaps one of the most important areas in the counseling field.

Área afectiva/emocional (vocabulario general)	Affective/emotional domain (general vocabulary)
Afecto	Affection/warmth
Alegre	Happy
Amor	Love
Ansioso/a	Anxious
Autoconsciente	Self-conscious
Conformista	Conformist
Confundido/a	Confused
Discapacidad mental	Mental disability
Dudar	To doubt

Emocionalmente dependiente	Emotionally dependent
Fatigado/a *(both cognitive and behavioral)*	Fatigued/tired
Funcionar	To work
Incómodo *(both cognitive and behavioral)*	Uncomfortable
Inseguro/a *(both cognitive and behavioral)*	Insecure
Ira	Rage/anger
Malhumorado/a	Grumpy/bad-tempered
Odio	Hate
Seguro/a *(both cognitive and behavioral)*	Secure
Sensible	Sensitive
Sentido/a	Sense (noun) heartfelt (adjective)
Sentido de culpabilidad	Feeling of guilt
Triste	Sad

Área psicomotora/conductual (Psychomotor/Behavioral Domain)

The psychomotor (behavioral) domain consists of actions that place primary emphasis on the neuromuscular or physical activities of the student (client) (Papalia, Wendkos, Duskin & Feldman, 2004). It encompasses all visible activities, verbal or non-verbal, in or outside the counseling office or classroom, with peers, adults, or parents, and any type of social interaction or behavior displayed or conducted alone. This is the easiest domain to deal with because it is visible and provides a window of observation into the other two domains: cognitive and affective. As you will have noticed, when dealing with your own or your client's struggles with language, the behavioral domain plays a critical part in the communication process and helps you determine whether or not the student understands what you are trying to communicate as you observe his or her body language.

🔊🎧

Área psicomotora/conductual (vocabulario general)	Psychomotor/behavioral domain (general vocabulary)
Agravar	Aggravate
Agresivo/a	Aggressive
Animado/a	Lively
Antisocial	Antisocial
Atento/a	Attentive
Callado/a	Quiet

Área psicomotora/conductual (vocabulario general)	Psychomotor/behavioral domain (general vocabulary)
Callar	To shut up
Dependiente	Dependent
Desatento/a	Inattentive
Desordenado/a	Disorderly
Destrezas académicas	Academic skills
Destrezas sociales	Social skills
Discapacidad física	Physical disability
Emotivo/a	Emotional
Energético/a	Energetic
Experto/a	Expert/adept
Falta de atención	Lack of attention
Hablador	Talkative
Impedimento	Impediment/disability
Independiente	Independent
Infantil	Infantile/childish
Inquieto/a	Restless
Interesado/a	Interested
Irrespetuoso/a	Disrespectful
Introvertido/a	Introverted
Lento *(both cognitive and behavioral)*	Slow
Llorar	To cry
Obstinado/a	Obstinate
Rápido *(both cognitive and behavioral)*	Fast
Renuente	Reluctant
Retante	Challenging
Rudo/a	Rude
Ruidoso/a	Noisy
Solitario/a	Solitary (a loner)
Suicida	Suicidal
Temperamental	Temperamental
Violento/a	Violent

Conducta de estudiantes (Students' Behavior)

This vocabulary associated with discipline and behavior is typically applied when a student has been referred by a teacher, school administrator, or parent.

Conceptos relacionados a la conducta negativa de estudiantes y asuntos de disciplina	Concepts related to students' negative behavior and discipline issues
Abandonar la escuela/deserción escolar	To drop out of school/school dropout
El abuso de las drogas	Drug abuse
El abuso verbal	Verbal abuse
Aconsejar	To advise/to counsel
Las actividades destructivas	Destructive activities
Las actividades peligrosas	Dangerous activities
Los actos obscenos	Obscene acts
La agresión física	Physical agression/assault
La agresión verbal	Verbal aggression/assault
Alcohol	Alcohol
Amenazar	To threaten
La asociación con pandillas	Gang affiliation
Las autoridades	Authorities
Bajo la influencia	Under the influence
Buena conducta	Good behavior
Las buenas decisiones	Good decisions
La campana de comienzo de clases	School bell
El castigo	Punishment
El centro de detención de menores	Juvenile detention center
El código de conducta	Code of conduct
Los comentarios racistas	Racist comments
El comportamiento vulgar	Vulgar behavior
La conducta desordenada	Disorderly conduct
Las consecuencias negativas	Negative consequences
Las consecuencias positivas	Positive consequences
La cultura de las drogas	Drug culture
Dañar	To damage/harm

Conceptos relacionados a la conducta negativa de estudiantes y asuntos de disciplina	Concepts related to students' negative behavior and discipline issues
El daño físico	Physical damage/harm
Desafiar la autoridad	To defy authority
Desobedecer	To disobey
La desobediencia	Disobedience
Destruir	To destroy
Destruir la propiedad escolar	To destroy school property
Disciplinar	To discipline
Un escándalo	Uproar/scandal
Escupir	To spit
Estropear	To damage/ruin
Faltar el respeto	To lack respect
Fumar	To smoke
Los gestos obscenos	Obscene gestures
Los grafiti	Graffiti
Ignorar las instrucciones	To ignore instructions
Una infracción menor	Minor offence
Interrumpir	To disrupt/interrupt
Irrespetuoso/a	Disrespectful
El lenguaje abusivo	Abusive language
Llegar a tiempo	To be on time
Llegar tarde	To be late
Mala conducta	Bad behavior
Las malas decisiones	Bad decisions
Las malas palabras/palabrotas	Swear words
Los malos hábitos de trabajo	Bad work habits
Mentir	To lie
Molestar a otros estudiantes	To annoy/disturb other students
Las pandillas	Gangs
El pandillero/miembro de la pandilla	Gang member
El pase de pasillo	Hall pass
La pelea a puños	Fistfight
El permiso	Permission

La policía	The police
La posesión de ...	Possession of ...
La posesión ilegal	Illegal possession
La propiedad pública	Public property
El programa de prevención de pandillas	Gang prevention program
Pegar	To hit
Peleando	Fighting
Pelear	To fight
La pérdida de material escolar	The losing of school work
Prohibido en terreno escolar/prohibido en la zona escolar	Prohibited on school grounds/prohibited at school
Las reglas escolares	School rules
Respetar	To be respectful
responsible	Responsible
Robar	To steal
Salir sin permiso	To leave without permission
Seguir las instrucciones	To follow instructions
Terminar la tarea	To complete homework
Tirar objetos	To throw objects
Tomar/beber alcohol	To drink alcohol
Usar drogas	To use drugs
El vandalismo	Vandalism
La violación de las reglas escolares	Violation of the school rules

Consecuencias típicas de la mala conducta	**Typical consequences of bad behavior**
La acción disciplinaria	Disciplinary action
La advertencia	Warning
La asistencia a la escuela de verano	Attendance at summer school
El aviso de bajas notas/calificaciones	Notice of poor grades
El aviso de mala conducta	Notice of bad behavior
La cita con el/la consejero/a académico/a	Appointment with the academic counselor
La cita con el principal	Appointment with the principal
Confiscar	To confiscate

Consecuencias típicas de la mala conducta	Typical consequences of bad behavior
Consecuencias académicas	Academic consequences
El contrato	Contract
El contrato de conducta	Behavioral contract
Estar expulsado	To be expelled
Estar suspendido/a	To be suspended
La notificación a los padres	Notification of parents
La pérdida del tiempo del recreo/receso	Loss of recess time
Responsable económicamente	Financially responsible
La reunión con los estudiantes	Meeting with the students
La reunión con los padres	Meeting with parents
Ser referido a la oficina	To be referred to the office
Trabajo académico adicional	Extra academic work

Estudiantes de necesidades especiales (Special Needs Students)

The following section tends to pertain more to school psychologists due to the evaluative nature of the terminology and the emphasis on the assessment of special needs students. However, it is customary for school counselors to also interact daily with these populations and their parents. Therefore, these terms have some relevancy to their daily activities as well.

Vocabulario relacionado con estudiantes de necesidades especiales y evaluación psicológica e intelectual	Vocabulary related to special needs students and psychological and intellectual evaluation
Adecuado	Adequate
Las actividades de enriquecimiento	Enrichment activities
El aliento/el ánimo	Encouragement
El análisis	Analysis
El aprendizaje	Learning
La aptitud	Aptitude

El arranque de cólera	Outburst
Asistir	To attend
El asesoramiento	Advice
La autodisciplina	Self-discipline
Bajo el promedio/inferior a la media	Below average
Calificar	To qualify
Cambios de estado de ánimo	Mood swings
La capacidad	Capacity
La clave	The key answer
La clínica del habla	Speech clinic
El cociente intelectual (CI)	Intelligence quotient (IQ)
La comprensión	Comprehension
El concepto negativo de sí mismo/a	Negative self-image
El concepto positivo de sí mismo/a	Positive self-image
La consecuencia	Consequence
Muy creativo/a	Very creative
El cuento	Story
El cuestionario	Questionnaire
Las debilidades	Weaknesses
La destreza	Dexterity
El detalle	Detail
Los dibujos	Pictures/artwork
Diferente	Different
Difícil	Difficult
Dificultad	Difficulty
Discapacidad de aprendizaje	Learning disability
Discutir	To discuss/argue
El dominio	Control/mastery
El dominio de sí mismo	Self-control
El lapso de atención	Attention span
La edad cronológica	Chronological age
La edad mental	Mental age
Los elogios	Praise
El error	Error
Espacial	Spatial

Vocabulario relacionado con estudiantes de necesidades especiales y evaluación psicológica e intelectual	Vocabulary related to special needs students and psychological and intellectual evaluation
Estado emocional	Emotional state
Estar al corriente	To be informed
El examen de selección	Screening test
El examen estandarizado	The standardized test
La expresión verbal/oral	Verbal/oral expression
Extenso	Extensive
La falta de atención	Lack of attention
Las fortalezas	Strengths
La frase	Phrase
El funcionamiento motor sensorial	Sensory motor functioning
La guía	Guide
Habilidades	Abilities/skills
La habilidad intelectual	Intellectual ability
Las habilidades básicas	Basic skills
El habla	Speech
Hablar	To talk
La hora establecida	Scheduled time
El horario	Schedule/timetable
El impedimento del habla	Speech impediment
Incompleto/a	Incomplete
Informar	To inform
El informe/reporte	Report
El informe escrito sobre el progreso	Written progress report
La instrucción asistida por computadora	Computer-assisted education
La instrucción básica	Basic education
Instrucción individual	Private tuition/lessons
Inteligencia	Intelligence
El interés	Interest
La intervención	Intervention
El leer los labios/la labiolectura	Lip reading

La lección	Lesson
Limitado	Limited
El logro	Achievement
El logro académico	Academic achievement
La memoria	Memory
La memoria auditiva	Auditory memory
Mínimo	Minimal
El mejoramiento	Improvement
La metodología	Methodology
Las necesidades excepcionales	Exceptional needs
El nivel del grado	Grade level
El nivel de lectura	Reading level
Las notas/calificaciones	Grades
La oración	Sentence
La práctica	Practice
La participación	Participation
Perder con la edad o el desarrollo	To outgrow
Solicitar una conferencia	Request a conference
El pensamiento creativo	Creative thinking
El pensamiento crítico	Critical thinking
La percepción	Perception
La personalidad	Personality
No satisfactorio	Unsatisfactory
El potencial	Potential
La preparación académica	Academic preparation
Los problemas auditivos	Auditory problems
Problemas físicos	Physical problems
El procedimiento	Procedure
El programa educativo individualizado	Personalized educational plan
El promedio	Average
El promedio de las notas	Grade point average
La pronunciación	The pronunciation
El recuerdo	Recall
La reevaluación	Reassessment
La rehabilitación del habla	Speech rehabilitation

Vocabulario relacionado con estudiantes de necesidades especiales y evaluación psicológica e intelectual	Vocabulary related to special needs students and psychological and intellectual evaluation
Repetir	To repeat
La respuesta	Answer
El resultado	Result/score/performance
Los resultados del examen… (ACT, SAT, ITBS, etc.)	Test/exam results of the … (ACT, SAT, ITBS, etc.)
Reunirse con…	To meet with …
El sonido	Sound
Satisfactorio	Satisfactory
Psicolingüístico/a	Psycholinguistic
Similar	Similar
El síndrome de falta de atención	Attention deficit syndrome
Sobre el promedio/superior a la media	Above average
La solución	Solution
Soñar despierto/a	To daydream
Superior al nivel del grado	Above grade level
Talentoso/a	Talented
La tarjeta de calificaciones	Report card
Tartamudear	To stutter/stammer
El temperamento	Temperament
La terapia del habla	Speech therapy
Las tutorías	Tutorials
El vocabulario	Vocabulary

Vocabulario escolar adicional (Additional School Vocabulary)

El salón de clases (vocabulario general)	The classroom (general vocabulary)
Las acuarelas	Watercolour paints
La alfombra	Carpet
El almacén	Storage room

El armario	Closet
El cesto de los papeles	Wastebasket
La carpeta	Folder
El centro de aprendizaje	Learning center
La cinta adhesiva	Scotch/adhesive tape
La computadora/el ordenador	Computer
Las cortinas	Curtains
Las crayolas/los crayones	Crayons
El crucigrama	Crossword puzzle
El libro de colorear	Coloring book
El cuaderno/la libreta	Notebook
El enchufe	Powersocket
La esponja	Sponge
El frasco	Jar
El gancho para ropa/el colgador	Coat hanger
La goma de borrar	Eraser
El pegamento/la cola de pegar	Glue
La grabadora	Tape recorder
La grapadora	Stapler
Las grapas	Staples
Las hojas de trabajo	Worksheets
El instrumento musical	Musical instrument
El interruptor de la luz	Electric switch
El juego	Game
El lápiz	Pencil
El librero/el estante de libros	Bookshelf
El libro	Book
El libro de audio	Audio book
El cuaderno de actividades	Workbook
El libro de texto	Textbook
Los materiales educativos	Teaching materials
La muñeca	Doll
La pantalla	Screen
El papel	Paper

El salón de clases (vocabulario general)	The classroom (general vocabulary)
La pared	Wall
El pincel	Paintbrush
Las pinturas	Paints
La pizarra/el pizarrón	Chalkboard
La plastilina/arcilla	Plasticine/clay
La pluma/el bolígrafo	(Ballpoint) pen
El proyector	Projector
La puerta	Door
La regla	Ruler
El reloj	Clock
El rompecabezas	Jigsaw puzzle
El salón	Classroom
El silbato/el pito	Whistle
La silla	Chair
El sobre	Envelope
El tablón de anuncios	Bulletin board
Las tarjetas	Flash cards
El termostato	Thermostat
Las tijeras	Scissors
Los títeres/las marionetas	Puppets
La tiza	Chalk
La ventana	Window

Carreras y selección de ocupaciones (vocabulario general)	Careers and occupational choices (general vocabulary)
Actuar responsablemente	To act responsibly
El apoyo de...	Support from ...
El apoyo de pares	Support from peers
El aprendizaje de nuevas destrezas	The learning of new skills

La ayuda financiera	Financial aid
La búsqueda de empleo de verano	The search for a summer job
El cambio de curso	Change of course
La carrera	Career
La colaboración	Collaboration
Auto conocimiento	Self-knowledge
La cooperación	Cooperation
Crecimiento personal	Personal growth
El curso	Course
Curso avanzado	Advanced course
Curso básico	Basic course
El desarrollo de un plan de acción	The developmentof an action plan
Las destrezas	Skills
Las destrezas ocupacionales	Occupational skills
El empleador	Employer
El empleo	Employment
La entrevista	Interview
La especialización académica	Academic major
La evaluación en línea	Online evaluation
El examen de admisión	Admission exam
Las formas	Forms
El futuro	Future
Las habilidades	Abilities
Inclinarse por…	To be inclined to…
La indecisión ocupacional	Occupational indecision
La identidad personal	Personal identity
La información	Information
La inseguridad	Insecurity
El interés	Interest
El inventario de intereses	Inventory of interests
El mercado laboral	Labor market
La ocupación	Occupation
La organización	Organization
La perseverancia	Perseverance

Carreras y selección de ocupaciones (vocabulario general)	Careers and occupational choices (general vocabulary)
El plan académico	Academic plan
La preferencia	Preference
Los requisitos	Requirements
Los requisitos mínimos	Minimum requirements
El resumen	Resume
Los resultados	Results
La selección	Selection
La selección de la especialización académica	The selection of an academic major
El sitio web	Website
La página web	Web page
La solicitud	Application
La solución	Solution
El/la supervisor/a	Supervisor
El tiempo libre/el ocio	Leisure
El trabajo	Work
El trabajador	Worker
El trabajo a tiempo parcial	Part-time job
La universidad	University
Valores personales	Personal values
La visión personal	Personal vision
Los valores personales	Personal values

La tarea escolar, tarjetas de calificación (notas) y conferencias con padres	School homework, report cards, and parents meetings
La calidad de estudio	Quality of study
La capacidad media/la capacidad promedio	Average ability
La cita	Appointment
Las consecuencias de las acciones	Consequences of actions

La dedicación	Dedication
La dedicación al estudio	Dedication to study
Entender la importancia de …	To understand the importance of …
Escoger un lugar para estudiar	To choose a place to study
Estudiar sin la televisión encendida	To study without the TV on
El éxito académico	Academic success
El fracaso académico	Academic failure
Los hábitos de estudio	Study habits
El lugar para estudiar	Place to study
Las metas del año académico	Goals for the academic year
Las metas del mes	Goals for the month
Las metas de la semana	Goals for the week
Las metas del semestre	Goals for the semester
Perseverancia	Perseverance
El promedio	Average
Los requisitos de la tarea	Homework requirements
La reunión importante	Important meeting
La situación preocupante	Worrying situation
La tarea	Assignment/homework
Las tareas no terminadas o incompletas	Incomplete homework
Las tareas terminadas	Completed homework
El tiempo para estudiar	Time to study
Las técnicas de estudio	Study techniques

Vocabulario de transporte en el autobús, el desayuno, el almuerzo, y la cafeteria escolar	**Vocabulary for bus transportation, breakfast, lunch, and the school cafeteria**
Agarrar/sostener	To hold
El agua	Water
El almuerzo gratis	Free lunch
El autobús escolar	School bus
La bandeja	Tray

Vocabulario de transporte en el autobús, el desayuno, el almuerzo, y la cafeteria escolar	**Vocabulary for bus transportation, breakfast, lunch, and the school cafeteria**
Beber	To drink
El boleto para el almuerzo	Lunch ticket
El basurero	Trash can
La cafetería	Cafeteria
La cajita del almuerzo	Lunch box
Caminar	To walk
La cola/la fila	Line/queue
La comida	Food
Las comidas gratis	Free meals
Comer	To eat
Comprar	To buy/purchase
La conducta en el autobús	Behavior on the bus
El/la conductor/a del autobús escolar	School bus driver
Correr	To run
Los cubiertos	Cutlery/silverware
La cuchara	Spoon
El cuchillo	Knife
Dentro del autobús	Inside the bus
Derramar	To spill
El dinero para comprar el almuerzo/desayuno	Lunch/breakfast money
Las estampillas para alimentos	Food stamps
Empezar/comenzar	To start
Empujar	To push
Esperar	To wait
Exento de pagar por el transporte escolar	Exempt from paying for school transportation
La falta de recursos para pagar	Inability to pay
Fuera del autobús	Outside the bus
Hacer fila para subir (al autobús)	To line up to get on (the bus)
Hora de recogida	Pick-up time

Jugo	Juice
Leche	Milk
Levantarse/pararse	To stand up
Limpiar	To clean
El lugar a donde ir	The place to go
El lugar de recogida	Pick-up point
El lugar para bajarse del autobús	Drop-off point
La mesa del almuerzo	Lunch table
La parada del autobús escolar	School bus stop
Pemanecer/quedarse	To stay
El plato	Plate
Poner	To put
El precio	Price
El precio del almuerzo/desayuno	Price of lunch/breakfast
El privilegio de viajar en el autobus escolar	Privilege of riding on the school bus
El programa de alimentos para niños/as	Child nutrition program
Querer	To want
Recoger/coger	To pick up/collect
La referencia de mala conducta en el autobús	Report of bad behavior on the bus
Las rutas	Routes
La salida de emergencia	Emergency exit
Sentar(se)	To sit down
El servicio de autobús	Bus service
La servilleta	Napkin
La solicitud para obtener transportación escolar	Application for school bus transportation
El sorbeto/la pajilla/el popote	Straw
La tarifa de transporte	Bus fare
La taza	Cup
El tenedor	Fork
Tirar	To throw
El/la trabajador/a de la cafetería	Cafeteria worker
El transporte en autobús	Bus transportation
La violación de las reglas de seguridad	The violation of safety rules

Vocabulario relacionada a la evaluación de la lectura y lenguaje (énfasis en Psicología Escolar)	Vocabulary related to the evaluation of reading comprehension and language (School Psychology Emphasis)
El acento	Accent
La actividad	Activity
La adivinanza	Riddle
El adverbio	Adverb
El alfabeto	Alphabet
El bosquejo	Outline
El capítulo	Chapter
La carta	Letter (correspondence)
La cita	Quotation
La coma	Comma
Comparable	Comparable
La comprensión	Comprehension
Las consonantes	Consonants
La conversación	Conversation
El cuento	Story
Los cuentos de hadas	Fairy tales
La descripción	Description
El diario/el periódico	Newspaper
El dicho	Saying
Las diferencias	Differences
La discusión	Discussion
El ejercicio	Exercise
El ensayo	Essay
La entrevista	Interview
Escrito/a	Written
La fábula	Fable
La gramática	Grammar
El habla	Speech
La idea	Idea

La imagen	Image
El informe oral	Oral report
La lectura	Reading
La lectura remediativa	Remedial reading
El lenguaje oral	Oral language
La letra mayúscula	Capital letter
Las letras	Letters (alphabetical)
El libro	Book
La línea de puntos	Dotted line
La lista	List
El margen	Margin
El material	Material
La narración	Narration
La oración	Sentence
Oral	Oral
Deletrear	To spell
La página	Page
La pausa	Pause
El plural	Plural
El poema	Poem
La poesía	Poetry
La pregunta	Question
El presente	Present
El punto	Period
El razonamiento	Reasoning
Las reglas	Rules
El resumen/el sumario	Summary
La rima	Rhyme
La secuencia	Sequence
Las semejanzas	Similarities
La sílaba	Syllable
El signo de interrogación	Question mark
El sinónimo	Synonym
El sonido	Sound

Vocabulario relacionada a la evaluación de la lectura y lenguaje (énfasis en Psicología Escolar)	Vocabulary related to the evaluation of reading comprehension and language (School Psychology Emphasis)
El sujeto	Subject
El tema	Theme
El texto	Text
El título	Title
La traducción	Translation
El verbo	Verb
El vocabulario	Vocabulary
La vocal	Vowel

Traditional educational and psychological assessments within school settings used to put more emphasis on the psychometric measurement of cognitive abilities and academic achievement. With time, evaluations of behavioral adjustment and personality were included. The diagnosis of a mental health condition is a serious matter, not least because it involves the eligibility of services of federal and state governments. Therefore, and considering the linguistic and cultural complexities involved, extreme caution is advised when working with a student who has a limited command of the English language.

Psicología Escolar (School Psychology)

Vocabulario relacionada al DSM-IV-TR (énfasis en Psicología Escolar)	Vocabulary related to the DSM-IV-TR (Diagnotic and Statistical Manual of Mental Disorder IV, Text Revised) (School Psychology Emphasis)
Las categorías	Categories
El daño a los demás	Harm to others
El desorden de la conducta	Behavioral disorder
El diagnóstico diferencial	Differential diagnosis

Eje I: Desórdenes clínicos y otras condiciones	Axis I: Clinical disorders and other conditions
Eje II: Desórdenes de personalidad y retardación mental	Axis II: Personality disorders and mental retardation
Eje III: Condiciones médicas generales	Axis III: General medical conditions
Eje IV: Problemas psicosociales y ambientales	Axis IV: Psychosocial and environmental problems
Eje V: Evaluación global del funcionamiento	Axis V: Global assessment of functioning
En remisión completa	In full remission
En remisión parcial	In partial remission
Excluir	To rule out/exclude
Las habilidades cognitivas	Cognitive abilities
Leve	Mild
Moderado	Moderate
Recuperado/a	Recovered
Severo	Severe
Los síntomas	Symptoms

DSM-IV-TR y síntomas de conducta disruptive/externalización de problemas (énfasis en Psicología Escolar)	DSM-IV-TR and symptoms of disruptive behavior/externalizing problems (School Psychology Emphasis)
El ajuste	Adjustment
Las expectativas de los otros y de la sociedad	The expectations of others and society
El historial crónico	Chronic history
Los patrones de conducta	Patterns of behavior
El patrón habitual	Habitual pattern
Peor	Worse
Persistente	Persistent
Romper las reglas	To break the rules
Serios disturbios emocionales	Serious emotional disturbances
Los síntomas crónicos	Chronic symptoms

DSM-IV-TR y síntomas de conducta disruptive/externalización de problemas (énfasis en Psicología Escolar)	DSM-IV-TR and symptoms of disruptive behavior/externalizing problems (School Psychology Emphasis)
El temperamento	Temperament
Comportándose mal	Behaving badly
Mejor con el tiempo	Better over time
La restricción de movimiento y actividad	Restriction of movement and activity
Emocionalmente perturbado	Emotionally disturbed
El desorden de conducta	Conduct disorder
La violación de las reglas principales	Violation of important rules
Acciones contra los derechos de otros	Actions against the rights of others
Negativo/a	Negative
Oposicional	Oppositional
Desafiante	Defiant
Permanecer afuera tarde por la noche sin el permiso del padre/madre/un guardián	To stay out late at night without permission from a parent/guardian
Intimidando a los demás	Intimidating others
El hurto en tiendas	Shoplifting
La pérdida de control	Loss of control
La agresión física	Physical assault
La destrucción de la propiedad	Destruction of property
Cualquier provocación	Any provocation
La distracción	Distraction
La hiperactividad	Hyperactivity
La falta de atención	Lack of attention
La impulsividad	Impulsivity
La adaptación del niño	Child's adjustment

Samples of Bilingual Charts and Scales

Charts and scales are excellent instruments that serve to enhance an evaluation process and speed up the recording of input from students during interviews. The utilization of pictures and diagrams provides a pictorial representation of some concepts without being necessarily intrusive. Since we have established that there is a wide range of variation among people with a Latin American background, measuring the level of acculturation is an important exercise that assists you in determining how closely aligned your students are to their culture of origin. Bilingual feeling and pain charts are particularly wonderful tools that can be used to represent the mood and level of physical discomfort of students at the moment of your interview with them. You can prompt your students' reactions without complex verbal explanation and can rely on pointing to the charts, which have bilingual definitions.

Working and Consulting with Parents

If you want to succeed in working with Latino/Hispanic youths, you MUST have their parents on your side! Remember that for the most part, first and second generation Latino/Hispanic youths think collectively and not as independent units; they rely on their parent's approval for many decisions that are normally made independently by the average US youth. There may be times when you will not have an interpreter at hand and you will have to deal with a new family yourself. Although you have to decide how comfortable you are with dealing with the parents and to what extent, the following provides you with a guideline for a basic interview.

Remember that many Latinos/Hispanics keep both the father's and mother's name (i.e. Juan Ruíz (father's) Castro (mother's)). Also, the mother, even when she is married, keeps her first maiden name and adds her husbands name after it using *de*, meaning literally "of" or "belonging to". For example, Carmen Castro *de* Ruíz.

Dates in Spanish are written in the following order: *day/month/year*. (e.g., 27 de enero de 2007).

Many Latino/Hispanic couples look after children who are not their own (e.g. nephews or children of a distant relative), raising them as though they were their own children. This may explain why some family members have different surnames.

Sample of a Parents' Interview

Nombre del padre *(Father's name)* _____

Fecha de nacimiento *(Date of birth)* _____

Ocupación *(Occupation)* _____

Teléfono del trabajo *(Work phone number)* ____-____-_____

Teléfono del hogar *(Home phone number)* ____-____-_____

Nombre de la madre *(Mother's name)* _____

Fecha de nacimiento *(Date of birth)* _____

¿Habla usted inglés suficientemente bien como para ayudar a su hijo/a con la tarea escolar? *(Do you speak English well enough to help your son/daughter with school homework?)*

Sí *(Yes)* _____   No *(No)* _____

Nombres de los/as niños/as y surelación familiar con usted(es) (ej., sobrino, ahijado) *(Names of children and their relationship to you (e.g. nephew, godson))*

Nombres *(Names)*	Edades *(Ages)*
a. _____	_____
b. _____	_____
c. _____	_____
d. _____	_____
e. _____	_____

¿Viven ustedes en una familiar nuclear o extendida? *(Do you live in a nuclear or extended family?)*

¿Cuáles son sus opiniones acerca de las tareas escolares? *(What are your opinions about school homework?)*

¿Por qué escogió está escuela para sus hijos/as? *(Why did you choose this school for your children?)*

¿Cuánto tiempo usted(es) dedica(n) a jugar con sus hijos/as? *(How much time do you dedicate to playing with your children?)*

¿Trabaja(n) usted(es) fuera del hogar? *(Do you work outside the home?)*

Si ambos trabajan, ¿quién cuida de sus hijos/as cuando ustedes no están en casa? *(If both of you work, who takes care of your children when you are not at home?)*

¿A quién están más apegados/as sus hijos/as? ¿Papá o mamá? *(Whom are your children closer to? Dad or mom?*

¿Fuman ustedes y/o consumen alcohol en la casa? ¿Fuera del hogar? *(Do you smoke and/or consume alcohol at home? Outside the home?)*

¿Cuáles han sido los eventos importantes o significativos durante el desarrollo de sus hijos/as? (ej. deportes, escuela, familia)? *(What important or significant events have there been throughout the development of your children?) (e.g. sports, school, family)?)*

¿Cuál ha sido un momento especial que le(s) hace recordar específicamente a sus hijos/as? *(What special momentsremind you of your children?)*

¿Qué es lo que usted(es) entiende(n) por el término "crianza ejemplar"? *(What do you understand by the term "exemplary parenting"?)*

¿Se ocupa usted por la dieta de sus hijos/as? *(Do you take care of your children's diet?)*

¿Cuáles son las comidas favoritas, y los colores, juguetes, juegos e intereses favoritos de sus hijos/as? *(What are your children's favorite foods, colors, toys, games and interests?)*

¿Qué cosas no les gustan a sus hijos/as? *(What things do your children dislike?)*

¿Cuál es la importancia de la educación? *(Why is education important?)*

¿Cuál fue el último regalo que le compró a sus hijos/as? *(What was the last gift you bought your children?)*

¿Cuál debe de ser el rol de los padres en la educación de sus hijos/as? *(What should be the parents' role in their children's education?)*

¿Cómo trabaja(n) usted(es) con la mala conducta de sus hijos/as? *(How do you deal with your children's bad behavior?)*

¿Cómo disciplina(n) usted(es) a sus hijos/as? (ej. Gritándoles/as, regañándoles/as severamente, conversando, golpeándoles/as, prohibiéndoles/as jugar, prohibiéndoles/as salir, humillándoles/as, encerrándoles/as en el cuarto.) *(How do you discipline your children? (e.g. yelling at them, scolding them severely, talking, hitting them, not allowing them to play, grounding them, humiliating them, locking them up in the bedroom.))*

¿Cree usted que los castigos son importantes en la vida? ¿Hasta qué punto? *(Do you believe that punishments are important in life? To what extent?)*

¿Qué quiere usted que sus hijos/as sean en el futuro? *(What would you like your children to be in the future?)*

¿Cuáles son sus expectativas para sus hijos/as? *(What are your expectations for your children?)*

¿Pelean ustedes o discuten mucho en la casa? ¿En frente de sus hijos/as? *(Do you fight or argue a lot at home? In front of your children?)*

¿Qué lengua hablan ustedes en casa? *(What language do you speak at home?)*

¿Cuán a menudo van a comer afuera? ¿Qué tipo de comida compran? *(How often do you go out to eat? What type of food do you buy?)*

¿Cuántas horas al día ven la televisión sus hijos/as? *(How many hours a day do your children watch TV?)*

¿Cuán independiente son sus hijos/as? *(How independent are your children?)*

¿Cómo se comporta sus hijos/as cuando conocen a un extraño? *(How do your children behave when they meet a stranger?)*

¿Tienen ustedes una computadora en la casa? *(Do you have a computer at home?)*

¿Están sus hijos/as al día en todas sus vacunas? *(Are your children up to date with their immunizations?)*

¿Sus hijos/asson introvertidos/as o extrovertidos/as? *(Are your children introverted or extroverted?)*

¿Cuántas veces a la semana usted(es) se dedican a conversar con sus hijos/as mientras la televisión está apagada? *(How many times a week do you have a conversation with your children while the TV is off?)*

Hábleme sobre su experiencia como padre/madre. *(Tell me about your experience as a parent.)*

¿Cree usted que sus hijos/as son felices? *(Do you think that your children are happy?)*

¿Qué necesidades especiales ha notado usted en sus hijos/as? *(What special needs have you noticed in your children?)*

¿Está usted de acuerdo de que sería beneficioso para sus hijos/as ver a un profesional de la salud mental? ¿Tiene objeciones sobre esto? *(Do you agree that it would be beneficial for your children see a mental health professional? Do you have any objections to this?)*

6   Substance Abuse Professionals

The prevalence of substance abuse issues permeating Latino/Hispanic groups in the US, including the abuse of alcohol and illegal drugs, has been linked to ethnocultural and socioeconomic factors that put many sectors of this population at risk (Straussner, 2001). Because Latinos/Hispanics differ markedly in terms of ethnic/racial background, socioeconomic status, political ideology, and cultural heritage, their experiences with substance abuse vary. For example, due to the fact that the majority of Cubans who arrived with the first wave of immigrants to the US had financial resources and education, their adaptation to the US economy, educational system, and society at large was smoother than for those who came illegally from Mexico or Central America with limited formal education and few resources (Straussner, 2001). Of course, a traumatic immigration experience, a particular ethnic background, and a low socioeconomic status will not always be undisputable indicators of a person's addictions or substance abuse, but rather will serve as general predictors.

An addiction is more than a behaviorial problem, since the repeated drug use causes long-lasting changes in the brain, which causes the addict to lose voluntary control. It is therefore critical that these behaviors are analyzed through a substance abuse filter as well as through the addict's cultural reality. Because long-term addiction alters the neurobiological processes of the brain, after prolonged use addicts will feel hopeless, helpless, and powerless, which makes their lives very complicated. If you consider that in the US about 50 percent of the population consumes alcohol and that one third of them will suffer a substance abuse disorder in their lifetime, then we are referring to an issue whose scope transcends cultures and ethnicities (SAMHSA, 2007).

Substance Abuse Terminology and Concepts

The next sections contain lists of some commonly used drugs and general terminology in the field of substance abuse:

Verbos asociados con abuso de sustancias y consejería en general que contienen raíces similares en ambos idiomas	Verbs associated with substance abuse and counseling in general that have similar roots in both languages (cognates)
Absorber	To absorb
Aceptar	To accept
Ajustar	To adjust
Alterar	To alter
Amputar	To amputate
Analizar	To analyze
Autorizar	To authorize
Calmar	To calm
Causar	To cause
Coagular	To coagulate
Concentrar	To concentrate
Considerar	To consider
Consistir	To consist
Constipar	To constipate
Consultar	To consult
Contaminar	To contaminate
Contener	To contain
Controlar	To control
Convertir	To convert
Cortar	To cut
Costar	To cost
Curar	To cure
Debilitar	To debilitate
Decidir	To decide
Declarar	To declare
Depender	To depend
Describir	To describe
Desinfectar	To desinfect
Destruir	To destroy
Diagnosticar	To diagnose

Dilatar	To dilate
Disolver	To dissolve
Distribuir	To distribute
Dividir	To divide
Eliminar	To eliminate
Esterelizar	To sterilize
Examinar	To examine
Fracturar	To fracture
Incluir	To include
Infectar	To infect
Inmunizar	To immunize
Inocular	To inoculate
Mantener	To maintain
Notar	To note
Observar	To observe
Obstruir	To obstruct
Orinar	To urinate
Penetrar	To penetrate
Preparar	To prepare
Prevenir	To prevent
Proceder	To proceed
Progresar	To progress
Prohibir	To prohibit
Prolongar	To prolong
Proteger	To protect
Purificar	To purify
Recuperar	To recuperate
Reducir	To reduce
Referir	To refer
Remediar	To remedy
Renovar	To renovate
Repetir	To repeat
Resucitar	To resuscitate
Resumir	To resume
Seleccionar	To select

Separar	To separate
Sufrir	To suffer
Transmitir	To transmit
Ulcerar	To ulcerate
Usar	To use
Visitar	To visit
Vomitar	To vomit

Vocabulario relacionado al abuso	Abuse-related vocabulary
Abstemio	Teetotaller (abstemious)
Abstinencia	Abstinence
Abstinencia condicionada	Conditioned abstinence
Abuso de analgésicos	Analgesic abuse
Abuso de antiácidos	Antacid abuse
Abuso de antidepresivos	Antidepressant abuse
Abuso de drogas	Drug abuse
Abuso de esteroides	Steroid abuse
Abuso de sustancias	Substance abuse
Consumo de alcohol abusivo/excesivo	Heavy/excessive drinking

Vocabulario general relacionado al alcohol y otros depresivos	General vocabulary related to alcohol and other depressants
Al-Anon	Al-Anon
Alcohol	Alcohol
Alcohol absoluto	Absolute alcohol
Alcohol de madera Metanol	Wood alcohol Methanol
Alcoholemia	Blood alcohol level (BAL)
Alcohólico/a	Alcoholic
Alcohólicos anónimos	Alcoholics anonymous
Alcoholismo	Alcoholism

Alcoholización	Alcoholization
Alucinosis alcohólica	Alcoholic hallucinosis
Barbitúrico	Barbiturate
Beber	To drink
Bebida alcohólica	Alcoholic beverage
Cirrosis alcohólica	Alcoholic cirrhosis
Consumo controlado de alcohol	Controlled drinking
Consumo de alcohol como escape	Drinking to forget
Consumo moderado de alcohol	Moderate drinking
Consumo de alcohol social	Social drinking
Control del alcohol	Alcohol control
Convulsiones relacionadas con el alcohol	Alcohol-related convulsions
Demencia alcohólica	Alcoholic dementia
Dependencia del alcohol	Alcohol dependence
Depresor	Depressant
Embriaguez	Drunkenness
Episodios de consumo intensivo de alcohol	Episodes of binge drinking
Etanol	Ethanol
Gastritis alcohólica	Alcoholic gastritis
Hepatitis alcohólica	Alcoholic hepatitis
Hijo de alcohólico	Child of an alcoholic (COA)
Impulso irresistible de beber	Craving to drink
Lesión cerebral inducida por el alcohol	Alcohol-related brain damage
Nivel de alcohol en la sangre	Blood alcohol level (BAL)
Pancreatitis alcohólica	Alcoholic pancreatitis
Paranoia alcohólica	Alcoholic paranoia
Persona adulta hijo/a de alcohólico	Adult child of an alcoholic
Resaca	Hangover
Síndrome alcohólico fetal (SAF)	Fetal alcohol syndrome (FAS)
Síndrome cerebral alcohólico	Alcoholic brain syndrome
Síndrome de dependencia del alcohol	Alcohol dependence syndrome
Tranquilizante	Tranquilizer
Trastorno psicótico inducido por el alcohol	Alcohol-induced psychotic disorder

Vocabulario general relacionado con los estimulantes	General vocabulary related to stimulants
Anfetamina	Amphetamine
Cafeína	Caffeine
Cocaína	Cocaine
Crack	Crack
Estimulante	Stimulant
Hojas de coca	Coca leaves
Nicotina	Nicotine
Psicosis por amfetaminas	Amphetamine psychosis
Tabaco sin humo	Smokeless tobacco
Tabaquismo pasivo	Passive smoking
Trastornos debidos al uso de tabaco	Tobacco-related disorders

Vocabulario general relacionado a las drogas alucinógenas	General vocabulary related to hallucinogenic drugs
LSD/Véase alucinógeno	LSD (lysergic acid diethylamide)
Mescalina	Mescaline
Peyote	Peyote
Planta alucinógena	Hallucinogenic plant
Polvo de ángel	Angel dust
Psicodélico	Psychedelic

Vocabulario general relacionado a las drogas opiáceas	General vocabulary related to opioid drugs
Codeína	Codeine
Heroína	Heroin
Metadona	Methadone
Morfina	Morphine
Opioide	Opioid

Vocabulario general relacionado a las cannabinoides	General vocabulary related to cannabinoids
Cannabis	Cannabis
Hachís	Hashish
Marihuana	Marijuana

Vocabulario general relacionado a las drogas farmacológicas	General vocabulary related to other pharmacological drugs
Antidepresivo	Antidepressant
Antihistamínico	Antihistamine
Droga anticonvulsivante	Anticonvulsant drug
Medicamento	Pharmaceutical drug/medication
Medicamento antiansiedad	Anti-anxiety drug/medication
Medicamento de libre dispensación	Over-the-counter drug/medication(OTC)

Vocabulario general relacionado a las adicciones y sustancias	General vocabulary related to addictions and substances
Abstinencia condicionada	Conditioned withdrawal
Adicción a las drogas o alcohol	Addiction to drug or alcohol
Administración (vía de)	Administration (method of)
Agente anoréxico	Anorexic agent
Agonista	Agonist
Amnesia	Amnesia
Amnesia aguda	Acute amnesia
Analgésico	Analgesic
Análisis de orina de drogas	Drug urinalysis
Cabeceo	Nodding
Centro de rehabilitación	Rehabilitation center

Codependiente	Codependent
Comorbilidad	Comorbidity
Compulsión	Compulsion
Comunidad terapéutica	Therapeutic community
Consumo de alcohol o drogas	Consumption/use of alcohol or drugs
Consumo controlado de drogas	Controlled drug use
Consumo de drogas	Drug use
Consumo de riesgo	Hazardous/high-risk use
Consumo experimental	Experimental use
Consumo perjudicial	Harmful use
Crear hábito	Habit-forming
Delírium tremens	Delirium tremens
Dependencia	Dependence
Desinhibición	Disinhibition
Desintoxicación	Detoxification
Detección de drogas	Drug testing
Deterioro del control	Impaired control
Diagnóstico dual	Dual diagnosis
Discapacidad relacionada con el alcohol o las drogas	Alcohol- or drug-related disability
Dopaje	Doping
Droga	Drug
Droga de diseño	Designer drug
Droga ilegal	Illicit drug
Droga legal	Licit drug
Embriaguez	Inebriation
Ebrio	Inebriate/intoxicated
Endorfina	Endorphin
Esnifar/oler pegamento	To sniff glue
Esteroides	Steroids
Facilitador	Facilitator/enabler
Grupo de autoayuda	Self-help group
Grupo de ayuda mutua	Support group
Habituación	Habituation
Imágenes retrospectivas	Flashbacks

Incapacidad de abstenerse	Inability to abstain
Inhalante	Inhalant
Inhibidor del apetito	Appetite suppressant
Instrumento diagnóstico	Diagnostic instrument
Intervención breve	Brief intervention
Intervención precoz	Early intervention
Intoxicación	Intoxication
Intoxicación aguda	Acute intoxication
Intoxicación patológica	Pathological intoxication
Laguna mental	Blackout
Legalización	Legalization
Mal viaje	Bad trip
Narcótico	Narcotic
Narcóticos anónimos	Narcotics Anonymous
Paranoia conyugal	Conjugal paranoia
Pérdida del control	Loss of control
Política farmacéutica	Pharmaceutical policy
Política de medicamentos	Medicines policy
Política en materia de drogas	Drugs policy
Potencial de dependencia	Potential for dependence
Predisposición al abuso	Predisposition for abuse
Prevención de la recaída	Prevention of relapse
Problema relacionado con drogas	Drug-related problem
Prohibición	Prohibition
Prueba diagnóstica	Diagnostic test
Psicofármaco	Psychopharmaceutical
Psicotrópico	Psychotropic
Reacción adversa a un medicamento	Adverse reaction to a drug/medication
Reacción idiosincrásica	Idiosyncratic reaction
Recaída	Relapse
Recuperación	Recovery
Reducción de daños	Harm reduction
Rehabilitación	Rehabilitation
Reinstauración	Reinstatement

Remisión espontánea	Spontaneous remission
Síndrome amotivacional	Amotivational syndrome
Síndrome de abstinencia	Withdrawal syndrome
Síndrome de dependencia	Dependence syndrome
Sobredosis	Overdose
Sobriedad	Sobriety
Sustancia/droga psicoactiva	Psychoactive drug/substance
Sustancias controladas	Controlled substances
Sustancias volátiles	Volatile substances
Tolerancia	Tolerance
Trastorno amnésico	Amnestic disorder
Trastornos por consumo de sustancias psicoactivas	Psychoactive substance-related disorders
Tratamiento de mantenimiento	Maintenance therapy
Usuario de drogas por vía intravenosa (UDVI)	Intravenous drug user (IVDU)
Uso compartido de agujas	Needle-sharing
Uso disfuncional	Dysfunctional use
Uso recreativo	Recreational use

Short- and Long-Term Effects of Substances

The following sections provide terminology related to alcohol, amphetamines, cocaine, heroin, inhalants, LSD, marijuana, nicotine, and PCP (phencyclidine) relative to their short- and long-term effects, and also some slang for which they are known.

Keep in mind that many factors control how an individual will respond to any drug. For instance, how the drug is taken or administered, its dosage, whether or not the drug is taken in conjunction with another drug, and the medical health of the person. In addition, there are unique factors that can alter the reaction of the individual to a drug. Among them are: age, sex, genetic predispositions, physical health, mental health, body weight, and percentage of body fat.

Alcohol

Efectos a corto plazo del alcohol	Alcohol's short-term effects
Aumento de frecuencia cardiaca	Increased heart rate
Cambios de estado de ánimo	Mood swings
Confusión	Confusion
Dilatación de vasos sanguíneos	Dilatation of blood vessels
Disminución de presión arterial	Lowering of blood pressure
Depresión de algunas áreas cerebrales	Depression of some brain areas
Falta de coordinación	Lack of coordination
Habla desorganizada	Disorganized speech
Pensamientos erráticos	Erratic thoughts

Efectos a largo plazo del alcohol	Alcohol's long-term effects
Contribuye a los efectos del cáncer	Contributes to the effects of cancer
Daño cerebral	Brain damage
Daño al hígado	Damage to the liver
Daño al páncreas	Damage to the pancreas
Daño al sistema nervioso	Damage to the nervous system

Jerga relacionada al alcohol	Slang related to alcohol
Agua caliente	Firewater
Bebida alcohólica	Booze
Caldo	Moonshine
Cóctel	Cocktail
Jugo	Juice
Licor	Liquor
Medicina	Medicine
Palo	Shot
Whisky soda	Highball

Anfetaminas

Efectos a corto plazo de las anfetaminas	Amphetamines' short-term effects
Ansiedad	Anxiety
Aumento de la frecuencia respiratoria	Increased breathing rate
Aumento del ritmo cardíaco	Increased heart rate
Aumento de la presión arterial	Increased blood pressure
Dilatación de las pupilas	Dilation of pupils
Disminución del apetito	Decreased appetite
Dolor de cabeza	Headache
Elevación de estado de ánimo	Mood elevation
Hiper alerta	Hyper alertness
Mareos/vértigos	Dizziness
Sequedad en la boca	Dry mouth
Sudoración	Sweating
Visión borrosa	Blurred vision

Efectos a largo plazo de las anfetaminas	Amphetamines' long-term effects
Deficiencias vitamínicas	Vitamin deficiencies
Dependencia	Dependency
Desnutrición	Malnutrition
Hiper alerta	Hyper alertness
Halucinaciones	Hallucinations
Ilusiones	Delusions
Paranoia	Paranoia
Pérdida de peso	Weight loss
Tolerancia	Tolerance
Úlceras	Ulcers

Jerga relacionada a las anfetaminas	Slang related to amphetamines
Corazones	Hearts
Cristal	Crystal
Hielo	Ice
Metanfetamina de cristal	Crystal meth
Pepas	Pep pills
Spid	Speed

Cocaína

Efectos a corto plazo de la cocaína	Cocaine's short-term effects
Desorientación	Disorientation
Marcha vacilante	Staggering gait
Pobre juicio	Poor judgment
Reflejos lentos	Slow reflexes
Relajación muscular	Muscular relaxation
Resaca	Hangover
Somnolencia	Sleepiness/drowsiness

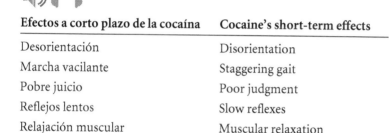

Efectos a largo plazo de la cocaína	Cocaine's long-term effects
Agitación	Agitation
Dependencia	Dependency
Intensificación de problemas emocionales subyacentes	Intensification of underlying emotional problems
Irritabilidad	Irritability
Paranoia	Paranoia
Tolerancia	Tolerance

Jerga relacionada a la cocaina	Slang related to cocaine
Amarillas	Yellows
Demonios rojos	Red devils
Downer	Downer
Dulce	Candy
Maníes	Peanuts
Rosas	Pinks

Heroina

Efectos a corto plazo de la heroína	Heroin's short-term effects
Alivio al dolor	Pain relief
Cambios de estado de ánimo	Mood changes
Confusión	Confusion
Depresión respiratoria	Respiratory depression
Disminución del apetito	Decreased appetite
Euforia	Euphoria
Mareos	Dizzness

Efectos a largo plazo de la heroína	Heroin's long-term effects
Anemia	Anemia
Deficiencia vitamínica	Vitamin deficiency
Desnutrición	Malnutrition
Indiferencia a la higiene personal	Indifference to personal higiene
Reducción de producción de la hormona masculine	Reduced production of male hormones
Tolerancia y dependencia	Tolerance and dependency
Vulnerabilidad a las infecciones y enfermedades	Vulnerability to infections and diseases

Jerga relacionada a la heroína	Slang related to heroin
Azúcar morena	Brown sugar
Brea negra	Black tar
Brea marrón	Brown tar
Lodo/fango	Mud
Nieve	Snow
Polvo blanco	White powder

Inhalantes

Efectos a corto plazo de los inhalantes	Inhalants' short-term effects
Alucinaciones	Hallucinations
Convulsions	Seizures
Delirio	Delirium
Dolor de cabeza	Headache
Euforia	Euphoria
Estornudos y tos	Sneezing and coughing
Falta de coordinación	Lack of coordination
Nausea	Nausea
Sensibilidad a la luz	Sensitivity to light
Visión borrosa	Blurred vision

Efectos a largo plazo de los inhalantes	Inhalants' long-term effects
Daño al hígado	Damage to liver
Daño a los riñones	Damage to kidneys
Depresión	Depression
Fatiga	Fatigue
Halitosis	Halitosis
Hostilidad	Hostility

Olvido	Forgetfulness
Paranoia	Paranoia
Sangrando por la nariz (hemorragia nasal)	Nosebleeds
Temblores	Trembling/shaking
Úlceras faciales	Facial sores

Jerga relacionada a los inhalantes	**Slang related to inhalants**
Gas de la risa	Laughing gas
Pega	Glue
Poppers	Poppers
Rush	Rush

Marihuana

Efectos a corto plazo de la marihuana	**Marijuana's short-term effects**
Aumento de apetito	Increased appetite
Aumento del ritmo cardíaco	Increased heart rate
Desorientación	Disorientation
Deterioro de la memoria	Memory impairment
Euphoria	Euphoria
Falta de coordinación	Lack of coordination
Irritación respiratoria	Respiratory irritation
Ojos rojizos/irritados	Red/irritated eyes
Somnolencia	Sleepiness/drowsiness

Efectos a largo plazo de la marihuana	**Marijuanas' long-term effects**
Daño pulmonar	Lung damage
Dependencia psicológica	Psychological dependence

Deterioro de la capacidad de aprendizaje	Impaired learning ability
Falta de energía y motivación	Lack of energy and motivation
Paranoia	Paranoia

Jerga relacionada a la marihuana	Slang related to marijuana
Mary Jane	Mary Jane
Oro de Acapulco	Acapulco gold
Pasto	Weed
Porro	Reefer
Yerba	Grass

LSD

Efectos a corto plazo del LSD	Short-term effects of LSD
Dilatación de las pupilas	Enlarged pupils
Disminución del apetito	Decreased appetite
Distorciones perceptuales (del placer al horror)	Perceptual distortions (from pleasure to horror)
Elevación de la temperatura corporal	Elevated body temperature
Escalofríos y sudoración	Chills and sweats
Latidos rápidos del corazón	Rapid heartbeat
Nausea	Nausea
Temblores	Trembling/shaking

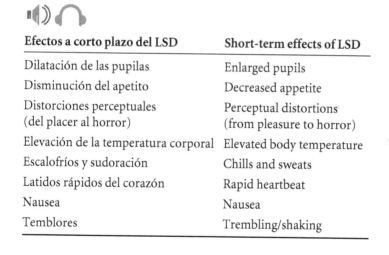

Efectos a largo plazo del LSD	Long-term effects of LSD
Agitación	Agitation
Alucinaciones al azar	Random hallucinations
Insomnia	Insomnia

Jerga relacionada al LSD	Slang related to LSD
Ácido	Acid
Azúcar	Sugar
Trip	Trip

Nicotina

Efectos a corto plazo de la nicotina	Short-term effects of nicotine
Acidez estomacal	Stomach acidity
Aumento de la presión arterial	Increased blood pressure
Aumento de ritmo cardíaco	Increased heart rate
Disminución del apetito	Decreased appetite
Disminución de la resistencia física	Diminished physical resistance to …
Disminución del sentido del gusto y el olfato	Reduced sense of taste and smell
Mal aliento	Bad breath

Efectos a largo plazo de la nicotina	Long-term effects of nicotine
Adicción	Addiction
Bronquitis crónica	Chronic bronchitis
Cáncer de esófago	Cancer of the esophagus
Cáncer de laringe	Cancer of the larynx
Cáncer de la cavidad oral	Cancer of the oral cavity
Cáncer de pulmón	Lung cancer
Descoloramiento y perdida de dientes	Discoloration and loss of teeth
Derrame cerebral	Stroke/brain hemorrhage
Enfisema	Emphysema
Enfermedades del corazón	Heart disease

Jerga relacionada a la nicotina	Slang related to nicotine
Pitillo	Cigs
Tabaco	Smoke
Tabaco de mascar	Chew

PCP

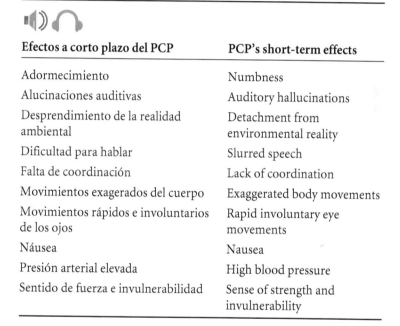

Efectos a corto plazo del PCP	PCP's short-term effects
Adormecimiento	Numbness
Alucinaciones auditivas	Auditory hallucinations
Desprendimiento de la realidad ambiental	Detachment from environmental reality
Dificultad para hablar	Slurred speech
Falta de coordinación	Lack of coordination
Movimientos exagerados del cuerpo	Exaggerated body movements
Movimientos rápidos e involuntarios de los ojos	Rapid involuntary eye movements
Náusea	Nausea
Presión arterial elevada	High blood pressure
Sentido de fuerza e invulnerabilidad	Sense of strength and invulnerability

Efectos a largo plazo del PCP	PCP's long-term effects
Aislamiento social	Social isolation
Ansiedad	Anxiety
Arrebatos de violencia	Violent outbursts
Depresión severa	Severe depression
Psicosis	Psychosis

Jerga relacionada al PCP	Slang related to PCP
Cerdo	Hog
Mala hierba	Killer weed
Polvo de angel	Angel dust

Interviews and Interventions

There are various types of interview formats and interventions that are currently used by many agencies and substance abuse professionals. This section will include a Spanish translation of the twelve steps for alcoholics anonymous, a short alcohol use evaluation, and a substance abuse history questionnaire. Two case studies follow these sections in order for you to see the use of various concepts from these generic instruments.

 Keep in mind that some Latino/Hispanic clients are partially bilingual and maybe able to understand the majority of the content of the English versions of some interview formats, but at times they may need clarification by using some Spanish concepts. This strategy is applicable to all sections of this book.

Los doce pasos originales de alcohólicos anónimos	The original twelve steps of alcoholics anonymous
1. Admitimos que éramos impotentes ante el alcohol; que nuestras vidas se habían vuelto ingobernables.	We admitted we were powerless over alcohol; that our lives had become unmanageable.
2. Llegamos a creer que un Poder superior a nosotros mismos podría devolvernos el sano juicio.	We came to believe that a Power greater than ourselves cold restore us to sanity.
3. Decidimos poner nuestras voluntades y nuestras vidas al cuidado de Dios, como nosotros lo concebimos.	We made a decision to turn our will and our lives over to the care of God as we understood Him.
4. Sin miedo hicimos un minucioso inventario moral de nosotros mismos.	We made a searching and fearless moral inventory of ourselves.
5. Admitimos ante Dios, ante nosotros mismos, y ante otro ser humano la naturaleza exacta de nuestros defectos.	We admitted to God, to ourselves, and to another human being the exact nature of our wrongs.

6. Estuvimos enteramente dispuestos a dejar que Dios nos liberase de nuestros defectos.	We were entirely ready to have God remove all these defects of character.
7. Humildemente le pedimos que nos liberase de nuestros defectos.	We humbly asked Him to remove our shortcomings.
8. Hicimos una lista de todas aquellas personas a quienes habíamos ofendido y estuvimos dispuestos a reparar el daño que les causamos.	We made a list of all the people we had harmed and became willing to make amends to them all.
9. Reparamos directamente a cuantos nos fue posible el daño causado, excepto cuando el hacerlo implica perjuicio para ellos o para otros.	We made direct amends to such people wherever possible, except when to do so would injure them or others.
10. Continuamos haciendo nuestro inventario personal y cuando nos equivocábamos, lo admitíamos inmediatamente.	We continued to make a personal inventory and when we were wrong, promptly admitted it.
11. Buscamos a través de la oración y la meditación mejorar nuestro contacto consciente con Dios, como nosotros lo concebimos, pidiéndole solamente que nos dejase conocer su voluntad para nosotros y nos diese la fortaleza para cumplirla.	We sought through prayer and meditation to improve our conscious contact with God as we understood Him, praying only for knowledge of His will for us and the power to carry that out.
12. Habiendo obtenido un despertar espiritual como resultado de estos pasos, tratamos de llevar el mensaje a los alcohólicos, y de practicar estos principios en todos nuestros asuntos.	Having had a spiritual awakening as a result of these steps, we tried to carry this message to alcoholics, and to practice these principles in all our affairs.

Evaluación Corta del Uso del Alcohol (Short Evaluation of Alcohol Use)

There are distinctive elements in the behavior of people who abuse a substance and have seen their daily lives affected in multiple areas. Typically it is family, friends, and work that are on the receiving end of alcohol abuse. Even if individuals are oblivious to their own erratic behaviors, the formulation of some key questions should elicit some degree of awareness. Now, since most instruments and sets of questions are based on self-reported answers, one must exercise caution with the analysis of these answers and in deciding how to proceed. The following are a set of short questions that will give you information pertinent to the substance abuse issue of the individual.

As a strategy to elicit awareness and the consequences of their own destructive actions, it is recommended that substance abuse counselors use the concept of family relationships to provoke insight. This is evident in the case of Luis Raúl (see Case Study 6).

Evaluación Corta del Uso del Alcohol	Short Evaluation of Alcohol Use
¿Piensa usted qué bebe cómo la mayoría de la gente?	Do you think that you drink like most people?
¿Qué le dicen sus amistades y familiares acerca de sus hábitos de la bebida?	What do your friends and family tell you about your drinking habits?
¿Ha asistido usted alguna vez a una reunión de un grupos de apoyo para el abuso de sustancias?	Have you ever attended a meeting for a substance abuse support group?
¿Cómo se han visto afectadas sus amistadas como resultado de sus patrones de bebida?	How have your friendships been affected as a result of your drinking patterns?
¿Le han dado en su trabajo alguna advertencia debido a su problema con la bebida?¿Ha faltado a su trabajo debido a la bebida?	Have you had a warning at work because of your drinking problem? Have you missed work because of drinking?
¿Ha visto alguna vez un doctor debido a la bebida?	Have you ever seen a doctor about your drinking?
¿Ha conducido alguna vez mientras está borracho? ¿Te han dicho tus amistades que no manejes porque están preocupados por ti?	Have you ever driven when drunk? Have your friends ever told you not to drive because they were concerned about you?

Historial de Abuso de Sustancias (Substance Abuse History)

The following questionnaire provides a general overview of clients' experiences with substances and how these have affected several areas of their lives. This is a generic questionnaire that can be easily adapted to any population. Many of these questions are addressed in the case of Karen, (See Case Study7) and Luis Raúl (See Case Study 6).

Generic Substance Abuse Questions—History

---

1. Al presente, ¿qué sustancias está consumiendo? Marque todoslos que apliquen. *(What substances are you currently using? Select all that apply.)*
   __alcohol *(alcohol)*__anfetaminas *(amphetamines/uppers)*
   __barbitúricos *(barbiturates/downers)*__cocaína *(cocaine)*
   __marihuana *(marijuana)* __nicotina *(nicotine (cigarettes/tobacco))*
   __inhalantes *(inhalants)*__LSD
   __PCP__heroína *(heroine)*
   __otros (hace una lista) *(others (list them))*
   _____

2. ¿Cuán frecuentemente consume usted estas sustancias? *(How frequently do you use these substances?)*
   __uso diario*(daily use)*
   __socialmente (ocasionalmente con amistades, en actividades, en fiestas) *(social use (occasionally with friends, during activities, at parties))*
   __fin de semana *(weekend use)*
   __uso ligero/livianamente (ocasionalemente, pero sin estar intoxicado o fuera de control) *(light use (occasionally, but without being intoxicated or out of control))*
   __uso intenso *(ocasionalmente hasta el punto de intoxicación y estar fuera de control) (heavy use (occasionally to the point of intoxication and being out of control))*

3. ¿Cuándo fue la última vez que usted consumió alcohol o drogas? *(When was the last time that you drank or used a drug?)* _____

4. ¿Durante los últimos tres meses ha consumido usted alcohol o drogas? Sí__ No__ *(Have you drunk or used drugs during the last 3 months? Yes__ No __)*

5. ¿Piensa usted que puede vivir sin el uso de alcohol o drogas? Sí__ No__*(Do you think that you can live without drinking or using drugs? Yes__ No __)*

6. ¿Puede usted dejar de consumir alcohol o drogas cuando usted lo desee? Sí__ No__*(Can you stop drinking or using drugs whenever you want to? Yes__ No __)*

7. ¿Usa usted drogas durante el día? Sí__ No__*(Do you use drugs during the day? Yes__ No __)*

8. ¿En qué lugares típicamente consume usted alcohol o drogas? Marque todos los que apliquen. *(Where do you typically drink or smoke? (Check all that apply.)*

__en mi hogar *(at home)*
__en la casa de un amistad *(at a friend's house)*
__en la casa de mi pareja *(at my partner's house)*
__en lugares públicos *(in public places)*
__en restaurantes y bares *(in restaurants and bars)*
__en reunions sociales *(at social gatherings)*
__ en fiestas *(at parties)*
__en otros lugares *(in other places)*

9. ¿Consumen alcohol y drogas la mayoría de sus amistades? Sí__ No__
    *(Do the majority of your friends drink alcohol and use drugs? Yes__ No
    __)*

10. ¿Con quién consume usted alcohol o drogas? *(Who do you drink or use
    drugs with?)*
    __con la familia *(with my family)*
    __con mi pareja *(with my partner)*
    __con mis amistades *(with friends)*
    __con extraños *(with strangers)*
    __con compañeros de trabajo *(with co-workers)*
    __solo/a*(alone)*

11. ¿Cómo considera usted su consumo? *(How do you consider your use?)*
    __liviano *(light)*
    __moderado *(moderate)*
    __intenso *(heavy)*

12. ¿Le dice su familia y amigos que usted está consumiendo demasiado?
    Sí__ No__*(Do your family and friends tell you that you are using too
    much? Yes__ No __)*

13. ¿Cómo compara usted su consumo con el de otros/as? Menos__Más
    o menosigual__Más__*(How do you compare your using with others?
    Less__About the same__More__)*

14. ¿Ha notado usted que sus hábitos de consumo de drogas y alcohol han
    cambiado últimamente? Sí__ No__*(Have you noticed that your drug
    use or drinking habits have changed lately? Yes__ No __)*

15. Como consecuencia de su consumo de drogas o alcohol usted: *(As a
    consequence of your drug use or alcohol consumption you:)*
    __ha perdido o tenido problemas en su trabajo *(have lost a job or have
    had problems at work)*
    __se ha comportado hostilmente o metido en peleas *(have been hostile
    or have been in fights)*
    __ha sido arrestado por conducer bajo los efectos de alcohol o drogas
    *(have been arrested for driving under the influence (DUI) of drink or
    drugs)*

__ ha sido arrestado debido a estar intoxicado en público *(have been arrested for being intoxicated in public)*

__ha perdido amistades or dañado relaciones familiares *(have lost friends or damaged family relationships)*

16. ¿Usted se ha arrepentido de sus acciones como consecuencia del consumo de alcohol y drogas? Sí__ No__Por favor explique.*(Have you regretted your actions as a result of your drug and alcohol use? Yes__ No __Sometimes__ Please explain.)*_____

_____

_____

17. ¿Cuáles son algunas de las razones por las cuales consume usted alcohol o drogas? Marque todos los que apliquen: *(What are some of the reasons that you use drugs or alcohol? Check all that apply:)*

__Yo consumo cuando estoy frustrado. *(I do it when I am frustrated.)*

__Yo consumo cuando estoy feliz. *(I do it when I am happy.)*

__Yo consumo cuando estoy enojado/a por alguna situación. *(I do it when I am angry about a situation.)*

__ Me gusta sentirme desconectado/a de mis problemas diarios. *(I like to feel disconnected from my daily problems.)*

__Me gusta consumir porque me brinda autoconfianza. *(I like to do it because it gives me self-confidence.)*

__Consumo porque me siento sin auto valía. *(I do it because I feel worthless.)*

__Consumo porque relaja mi mente y mi cuerpo. *(I do it because it relaxes my mind and body.)*

__ Consumo porque me torna más social y alegre. *(I do it because it makes me more sociable and happy.)*

__Consumo parque se lleva mis sentimientos de auto-derrota. *(I do it because it takes away my feelings of self-defeat.)*

__Consumo porque trabajo y hago mejor las cosas en general. *(I do it because I work and do things better in general.)*

18. Durante los últimos tres meses ¿ha intentado de detener el consumo de alcohol o drogas? Sí__ No__En caso afirmativo, por favor explique. *(During the last three months have you attempted to stop drinking or using drugs? Yes__ No __If so, please explain.)*

_____

19. ¿Ha conversado usted con otros en relación a su consumo de alcohol y drogas? Sí__ No__. Si lo ha hecho, ¿cuál ha sido el resultado? *(Have you talked to others about your consumption of drink or drugs?) Yes__ No __ If so, what was the outcome?)*_____

20. ¿Ha participado usted en el pasado en algún grupo de apoyo para el consumo de alcohol y drogas? Sí__ No__ *(Have you ever participated in a support group for drug or alcohol use? Yes__   No __)*

21. ¿Quiere usted ayuda profesional y apoyo familiar en relación de su consumo de alcohol y drogas? Sí__ No__ *(Do you want professional help and family support for your drug or alcohol use? Yes__   No __)*

Case Study 6: Luis Raúl (a substance abuse intervention).

(Note: This interview uses a generic pattern of questions based on the substance abuse questionnaire and the short evaluation of alcohol use instruments mentioned before. None of the questions have been tested under research conditions for reliability or statistical significance. However, their main purpose is to elicit awareness of substance abuse and to provide bilingual guidance to the substance abuse professional (SAP)).

Counseling context: Luis Raúl's wife (Soledad), their 14-year-old daughter (Tamara), and some family members and friends are waiting for Luis Raúl to arrive home from work. Soledad has arranged an intervention plan with you (an SAP counselor) because life has been intolerable during the last couple of years for the family. Luis Raúl has been missing work lately, has been abusive at home, and was arrested last week for being intoxicated in public. You summoned all of them at Luis Raúl's house and will start an intervention. After the initial shock of being "cornered" by everybody in his own home, Luis Raúl agrees to speak with you, the family members, and friends. *(La esposa de Luis Raúl (Soledad), su hija de 14 años (Tamara) y algunos miembros de la familia y amistades se encuentran en la casa esperando la llegada de Luis Raúl del trabajo. Soledad ha organizado un plan de intervención con usted (un/a consejero/a profesional de abuso de sustancias (PAS)) porque su vida se ha tornado intolerable durante el último par de años. Luis Raúl se ha ausentado de su trabajo últimamente, se ha comportado abusivamente en el hogar, y fue arrestado la semana pasada por estar intoxicado en público. Usted convocó a todos los familiares y amigos en la casa de Luis Raúl y comenzará una intervención. Luego de la primera impresión de sentirse "acorralado" por todos en su propia casa, Luis Raúl accede a hablar con usted, los miembros de la familia, y los amistades.)*

SAP*(PAS):*   I know that it must be very difficult for you to be surrounded by family, friends, and a complete stranger in your home after a long day at work. Your loved ones are very concerned about your well-being due to your alcohol use during the last year and how much you have changed. *(Yo sé que debe ser muy difícil para usted el estar rodeado de familiares, amigos, y ante un completo extraño en su hogar luego de haber tenido un largo día de trabajo. Sus seres queridos están muy preocupados por su bienestar debido a su abuso del alcohol durante el último año y lo mucho que ha cambiado.)*

Luis Raúl: This is completely ridiculous! First of all, I find it very offensive. Who gave you the right to be here? I pay the mortgage of this house, not my wife or daughter, and I decide who comes into my house. *(¡Esto es completamente ridículo! Antes que nada, lo encuentro muy ofensivo. ¿Quién le dio a usted el derecho de estar aquí? Yo pago la hipoteca de esta casa, no mi esposa o mi hija, y yo decido quien viene a mi casa.)*

SAP(PAS):   You are absolutely correct. You are the owner of this property and you decide who comes into your property. I am very grateful that you are listening to me, but I want to remind you that I am speaking for your family and friends. I am only a voice who is sending you a message. The message from your family and friends is: We love you, we are concerned about you, and we don't recognize our father, husband, and friend anymore. We are losing you to a substance, and alcohol is robbing us of a loved one. *(Usted está absolutamente correcto. Usted es el dueño de esta casa y es usted quien determina quién puede entrar en ella. Yo estoy muy agradecido/a de que usted me esté escuchando, pero le recuerdo que estoy hablando por sus familiares y amigos. Yo soy solo una voz que le está enviando a usted un mensaje. El mensaje de su familia y amistades es: Te amamos, estamos preocupados por ti, y ya no podemos reconocer más a nuestro padre, esposo y amigo. Te estamos perdiendo por una sustancia, y el alcohol nos está robando un ser querido.)*

Luis Raúl: [Sobbing in a state of semi-denial.] I understand that I have changed a little lately, but I have a lot of things going on. I am very concerned about work, paying the bills, saving money, and the fear of losing my job. Many co-workers have been laid off lately. *([Sollozando en un estado de negación parcial.] Yo entiendo que he cambiado un poco últimamente, pero es que tengo muchas cosas a la misma vez. Estoy muy preocupado por el trabajo, el pagar las cuentas, ahorrar dinero, y el miedo de perder mi trabajo. Varios trabajadores han sido despedidos últimamente.)*

SAP(PAS):   All of those are valid concerns and it must be difficult to deal with all these external pressures that increase your stress. *(Todas esas son preocupaciones muy válidas y debe ser muy difícil el tra-*

	tar de lidiar con todas esas presiones externas que incrementan su tensión.)
Luis Raúl:	Of course it is! It's damn hard! *(¡Diablos, claro que sí! ¡Es muy difícil!)*
SAP *(PAS)*:	Because your family and friends love you and do not want these valid problems and concerns to get out of control, they are concerned about how you are coping with the situation. *(Porque su familia y amigos le aman y no quieren que todas estas preocupaciones y problemas validos le lleven a perder el control, están preocupados por la manera en la cual usted le hace frente a la situación.)*
Luis Raúl:	What do you mean coping? *(¿Qué quiere usted decir con hacer frente?)*
SAP *(PAS)*:	Well, there are many ways to deal with daily life and occupational pressures. Some people talk about it with others, go outdoors for long walks or runs, go to church, visit a counselor or psychologist, create alternative occupational plans or attend a community college to enhance their occupational skills. How are you coping with your daily stresses? *(Bueno, hay muchas formas para lidiar con la vida diaria y presiones laborales. Algunas personas hablan acerca de ello con otros, salen al aire libre para caminar o a correr, asisten a la iglesia, visitan a un consejero o psicólogo, crean planes laborales alternativos o asisten a un colegio de la comunidad para mejorar sus destrezas laborales. ¿Cómo le hace frente usted a esos factores de tensión diarios?)*
Luis Raúl:	Well, I do talk with some people at the bar … *(Bueno, yo hablo con algunas personas en la barra …)*
SAP *(PAS)*:	Oh, okay. And do you believe that these conversations have been productive and have helped you? *(Oh, está bien. Y ¿usted cree que estas conversaciones han sido productivas y le han ayudado?)*
Luis Raúl:	[With a smirk on his face.] Not really. Most of them are on the same boat as me and drunk. *([Con una sonrisa en su cara.] No realmente. La mayoría de ellos están en el mismo bote que yo y borrachos.)*
SAP *(PAS)*:	Exactly. Perhaps they are not the best influence and source of assistance because they are intoxicated and their judgment is blurred. Have you talked to any of the people who are here with you? Some of these friends? *(Exactamente. Quizás ellos no sean la mejor influencia y fuente de asistencia porque están intoxicados y su juicio está borroso. ¿Ha hablado usted con algunas de las personas que están aquí ahora mismo con usted? ¿Algunos de estos amigos?)*
Luis Raúl:	No, not really. They are busy working and doing their own thing. *(No, no realmente. Ellos están ocupados trabajando y haciendo sus propias cosas.)*

SAP*(PAS)*: Perhaps is true, but have you attempted to contact them at some point? *(Tal vez sea cierto, ¿pero ha intentado usted contactarlos en algún momento?)*

Luis Raúl: No. So where are you going with this? *(No. Bueno, ¿a dónde quiere ir con esto?)*

SAP*(PAS)*: I know that it is difficult to handle certain things and this may be one of them. The situation is that unlike the acquaintances from the bar, these are your true friends who care about you and want the best for you. Have you noticed that your behavior has changed in the last six months? *(Yo sé que es muy difícil manejar algunas cosas y esta puede ser una de ellas. La situación es que a diferencia de los conocidos de la barra, estos son sus verdaderos amigos que se preocupan por usted y quieren lo mejor para usted. ¿Ha notado usted que su conducta ha cambiado en los últimos seis meses?)*

Luis Raúl: Not really. Well, maybe I've been getting home late and have missed work a couple of times. *(En realidad no. Bueno, a lo mejor he estado llegando a la casa un poco tarde y he faltado al trabajo varias veces.)*

SAP*(PAS)*: Occasionally, when we are unable to control alcohol consumption, our lives change to the point when everything gets out of control and one does not notice it, but everyone around us does. *(Ocasionalmente, cuando no somos capaces de controlar el consumo de alcohol, nuestras vidas cambian a tal punto cuando todo se sale de control y nosotros no lo notamos, pero los que están a nuestro alrededor sí lo notan.)*

Luis Raúl: Are you saying that I am a stinking drunk? *(¿Está usted diciendo que yo soy un borracho asqueroso?)*

SAP*(PAS)*: No, your family is saying that you have an issue with alcohol that needs to be remediated soon or you will get to the point of losing everything that you love. If you continue this pattern of consumption and behaviors you will lose your wife, daughter, job, house, and friends. You will end up alone and destroying your life and affecting the lives of those around you. Is this what you want for you and your loved ones? *(No, su familia está diciendo que usted tiene una situación con el alcohol que tiene que ser remediada muy pronto o usted llegara a un punto en el cual perderá todo lo que ama. Si usted continúa estepatrón de consumo y conductas usted perderá a su esposa, hija, trabajo, casa, y amigos. Usted terminará solo y destruyendo su vida y afectando la vida de todos a su alrededor. ¿Es esto lo que usted quiere para ustedy sus seres amados?)*

Luis Raúl: [Crying.] I just need some help. I think that I can stop drinking at any time. *([Llorando.] Yo solo necesito un poco de ayuda. Yo creo que puedo dejar de beber en cualquier momento.)*

SAP*(PAS)*:   I am glad to hear that you realize that you need some help. However, your wife and daughter told me that you tried to stop drinking and you didn't succeed. What you have is an addiction and you need professional help. *(Me alegra el escuchar que se da cuenta que necesita ayuda. Sin embargo, su esposa e hija me han dicho que usted ha intentado dejar de beber y no sucedió. Lo que usted tiene es una adicción y usted necesita ayuda profesional.)*

Luis Raúl: What do you mean by professional help? People like you? *(¿Qué quiere usted decir con ayuda profesional? ¿Personas cómo usted?)*

SAP*(PAS)*:   My agency provides medical and psychological assistance to help you succeed in the fight against your addiction. This is a battle that has to be fought on different fronts and using all possible resources. *(Mi agencia provee asistencia médica y psicológica para ayudarle a ser exitoso en contra de la adicción. Esta es una guerra que tiene que ser peleada desde diferentes frentes y utilizando todos los recursos posibles.)*

Luis Raúl: But if I go to a clinic, then I will lose my job, and I cannot afford to lose my job. *(Pero si voy a una clínica, entonces perderé mi trabajo, y yo no puedo darme el lujo de perder el trabajo.)*

SAP*(PAS)*:   You will not lose your job. In fact, your company pays for the rehabilitation services through your medical insurance; you don't have to worry about it. *(Usted no perderá su trabajo. De hecho, su compañía paga por los servicios de rehabilitación a través de su seguro médico; usted no tiene que preocuparse por esto.)*

Luis Raúl: I feel like a loser who can't control his damned booze. I'm a total failure … *(Me siento como un perdedor quien no puede controlar su maldita bebida. Soy un fracaso total …)*

SAP*(PAS)*:   You are not a loser. You are a normal human being who is struggling with an addiction. You are more than the addiction; the alcohol and the addiction are just parts of you, not you. Do you want to regain your life and avoid losing everything? Tell me. *(Usted no es un perdedor. Usted es un ser humano normal quien está luchando con una adicción. Usted es más que una adicción; el alcohol y la adicción son solo partes de usted, no son usted. ¿Quiere usted recuperar el control de su vida y evitar perderlo todo? Dígame.)*

Luis Raúl: Yes … I do. I am so sorry for all that I have done to all of you … *(Sí … Yo quiero. Yo siento mucho todo lo que les he hecho a todos ustedes …)*

SAP*(PAS)*:   Please, follow me. We will go through this part of your journey together. *(Por favor, sígame. Nosotros vamos a pasar por esta parte de su camino juntos.)*

Case Study 7: Karen (a general substance abuse interview for adolescents).

(Note: This interview uses a generic pattern of questions based on the substance abuse questionnaire and the short evaluation of alcohol use instruments mentioned before. None of the questions have been tested under research conditions for reliability or statistical significance. However, the main purpose of these questions is to elicit awareness relative to substance abuse and to provide bilingual guidance to the SAP).

Counseling context: Karen is an 18-year-old youth and a second generation Honduran who lives in Chicago. According to an interview with her parents via an interpreter, Karen's behavior has substantially changed during the last two years. The parents reported that she has been "influenced" by some kids who are affiliated with the Latin Kings (a street gang) in the neighborhood. Her grades have dropped significantly and she has been suspended for fighting twice. The parents suspect that Karen is smoking marijuana because sometimes she comes home with a "strange and peculiar smell." Karen was referred to your substance abuse agency by the school counselor. As a substance abuse counselor, you want to render a tentative diagnosis relative to her drug and alcohol use in order to execute a formal battery of evaluation. *(Karen es una joven de 18 años de edad y una hondureña de segunda generación que vive en Chicago. De acuerdo con una entrevista con sus padres a través de un intérprete, la conducta de Karen ha cambiado sustancialmente durante los últimos dos años. Los padres reportaron que ella ha sido influenciada por algunos chicos del barrio que están afiliados a los Latin Kings (una pandilla). Sus calificaciones han decaído sustancialmente y ha sido suspendida de la escuela dos veces por pelearse. Los padres sospechan que Karen está fumando marihuana porque a veces llega a casa con un "olor extraño y peculiar." Karen fue referida a su agencia de control de abuso de sustancias por un consejero escolar. Como consejero/a profesional de abuso de sustancias usted desea hacer un diagnóstico provisional en relación al abuso de alcohol y otras sustancias para entonces ejecutar una batería formal de evaluación.)*

SAP*(PAS)*:   Good morning Karen, how are you today? *(Buenos días Karen, ¿cómo estás hoy?)*

Karen: Okay. *(Bien)*

SAP*(PAS)*:   I just want to remind you that my role is to help you. As a professional, I want the best for you. That's all. *(Solo deseo recordarte que mi rol es el ayudarte. Como profesional, yo deseo lo mejor para ti. Eso es todo.)*

Karen:	Yes, but my parents are really pushy. *(Sí, pero mis padres son muy agresivos.)*
SAP*(PAS)*:	Let's concentrate on what's best for you, just you, at this point. We can talk about your parents later on as we progress with our interview. Okay? *(En este momento, vamos a concentrarnos en lo que es mejor para ti, solo ti. Luego podemos hablar sobre tus padres a medida que avancemos con la entrevista. ¿Está bien?)*
Karen:	All right. *(Muy bien).*
SAP*(PAS)*:	The only thing that I am going to ask for is for your honesty and sincerity, otherwise I will not be able to help you in any way. *(La única cosa que yo te voy a pedir es tu honestidad y sinceridad, de otra forma yo no voy a poder ayudarte de ninguna manera.)*
Karen:	Fine. But are you going to tell my parents everything? *(Está bien. ¿Pero usted le va a decir todo a mis padres?)*
SAP*(PAS)*:	That's an excellent question, Karen. I will be honest with you. I am bound by the ethics of confidentiality, which means that I cannot disclose the content of our conversations or reveal the results of any test with your parents. Even though you are living with your parents, you are an adult according to the law. However, if you attempt to hurt yourself or disclose that you are planning to do so, or to hurt someone, then I am mandated by law to report it and disclose the situation. *(Esa es una pregunta excelente, Karen. Voy a ser honesto/a contigo. Yo estoy atado/a a la ética de confidencialidad, que significa que yo no puedo revelar a tus padres el contenido de nuestras conversaciones o los resultados de cualquier examen. A pesar de que tú estás viviendo con tus padres, tú eres un adulto según la ley. Sin embargo, si tu intentas hacerte daño o revelas planes en torno a esto o a hacer daño a alguien, entonces estoy obligado/a por ley a reportarlo y revelar la situación.)*
Karen:	No, no. I am not thinking about killing myself. I am not stupid or crazy! *(No, no. Yo no estoy pensando en matarme.¡Yo no soy estúpida o loca!)*
SAP*(PAS)*:	I know that you are a very intelligent and sensitive young woman, but it is my obligation to inform you of the limitations of confidentiality. All right? *(Yo sé que tú eres una joven muy inteligente y sensible, pero estoy obligada a informarte de las limitaciones de la confidencialidad. ¿Está bien?)*
Karen:	I understand. *(Lo entiendo.)*
SAP*(PAS)*:	Now, out of respect to your parents and because they care for you and are concerned about your well-being, perhaps later on you and I can come up with a plan of how much informa-

tion you want to tell your parents. I will be more than glad to be part of the conversation. However, we can leave this issue for later and should concentrate on you for now. *(Ahora, por respeto a tus padres y porque ellos se preocupan por ti y están preocupados por tú bienestar, quizás luego tú y yo podemos hacer un plan sobre cuanta información tú le quieres decir a tus padres. Estaré más que contento/a de tomar parte en la conversación. Sin embargo, podemos dejar este asunto para más tarde y debemos concentrarnos en ti por ahora.)*

Karen: Sounds good to me. *(Me suena bien.)*

SAP*(PAS)*:   Let's start with some questions. What kind of drugs are you using? *(Vamos a comenzar con algunas preguntas. ¿Qué tipo de drogas estás usando?)*

Karen: Does drinking count? *(¿El beber cuenta?)*

SAP*(PAS)*:   Yes, it does count. *(Sí, cuenta.)*

Karen: Well, in that case, booze, pot, and I have tried a couple of uppers with beer. Oh, and cigarettes, but those are not drugs, right? *(Bien, en ese caso, alcohol, pasto/yerba, y también he probado un par de pastillas con cerveza. Ah, y cigarrillos, pero esos no son drogas, ¿verdad?)*

SAP*(PAS)*:   First, thanks so much for your honesty. And let me see if I am following you. So you have used alcohol, marijuana, amphetamines, and tobacco. Correct? *(Primeramente, muchas gracias por tu honestidad. Y déjame ver si estoy siguiéndote. O sea, tú has consumido alcohol, marihuana, anfetaminas y tabaco. ¿Correcto?)*

Karen: I guess that those are the "proper" names of what I have used. *(Karen: Supongo que esos son los nombre "correctos" de lo que he usado.)*

SAP*(PAS)*:   There are no proper or wrong names, I just wanted to make sure that we were talking about the same things. You are doing very well. Let's continue. So how often do you use these drugs? Think on a daily and weekly basis. *(No hay nombres correctos o incorrectos, yo solo quería estar seguro/a de que estábamos hablando de las mismas cosas. Tú lo estás haciendo muy bien. Continuemos. Entonces, ¿cuán frecuentemente usas esas drogas? Piensa en esto de forma diaria y semanal.)*

Karen: Well, I smoke four or five cigarettes a day, maybe two or three joints a day, and a couple of beers. I tried the uppers a couple of times but they kicked me too hard and I have not tried them since. *(Bueno, yo me fumo cuatro o cinco cigarrillos al día, quizás dos o tres pitillos cada día, y un par de cervezas. He tratado las pastillas un par de veces pero ellas me patearon muy fuerte y no las he probado más.)*

SAP*(PAS)*:   So when was the last time you smoked marijuana and drank beer? *(Bien, ¿cuándo fue la última vez que fumaste marihuana y tomaste cerveza?)*

Karen: Yesterday night with some friends in the park. *(Ayer por la noche con algunos amigos en el parque.)*

SAP*(PAS)*:   Have you smoked and drunk almost daily during the last two or three months? *(¿Has fumado y bebido casi diariamente durante los últimos dos o tres meses?)*

Karen: Oh yeah, definitely; maybe the last six or eight months. I am not sure though. *(Oh sí, seguro; quizás los últimos seis u ocho meses. Pero no estoy segura.)*

SAP*(PAS)*:   Do you think that you could handle a day without smoking or drinking or would it be too hard? *(¿Crees que podrás manejar un día sin beber o fumar? ¿Osería muy difícil?)*

Karen: I don't know, I guess that I'm used to it. It relaxes me and helps me to deal with daily crap. *(Yo no sé, creo que estoy acostumbrada. Me relaja y me ayuda a lidiar con la mierda diaria.)*

SAP*(PAS)*:   It sounds like you are having a rough time and you more or less need to smoke and drink in order to cope with your daily problems. *(Parece que estás pasando por un momento difícil y más o menos necesitas fumar y beber para manejar tus problemas diarios.)*

Karen: Yeah. *(Sí).*

SAP*(PAS)*:   Can you stop smoking and drinking whenever you want? *(¿Puedes dejar de fumar cuando quieras?)*

Karen: I don't know, I guess so. But I tried one time and felt kind of sick and too tense ... *(No sé, supongo que sí. Pero traté una vez y me sentí enferma y muy tensa ...)*

SAP*(PAS)*:   I see. Where and when do you usually smoke and drink? *(Ya veo. ¿Dónde usualmente fumas y bebes?)*

Karen: Behind the school building and at the park at night. I can't smoke or drink at home because my parents and my little brother and sister are always there. *(Detrás del edificio de la escuela y en el parque por la noche. No puedo fumar en mi casa porque mis padres, mi hermanita y hermanito siempre están allí.)*

SAP*(PAS)*:   Alone or with your friends? *(¿Sola o con tus amigos?)*

Karen: With my friends. But sometimes I have done it alone in the park. *(Con mis amistades. Pero a veces lo he hecho sola en el parque.)*

SAP*(PAS)*:   Do all the friends that you hang out with tend to smoke and drink? *(¿Todas las amistades con las que frecuentas tienden a fumar y beber?)*

Karen:	Yeah. Melinda was my best friend but since she does not smoke or drink, I don't hang out with her anymore. Well, actually she doesn't want to be with me because of my other friends. *(Sí. Melinda era mi mejor amiga pero ya que ella no fuma or bebe, ya yo no salgo con ella. Bueno, en realidad ella no quiere estar conmigo debido a mis otras amistades.)*
SAP*(PAS)*:	Do your friends belong to a gang? *(¿Tus amistades pertenecen a una pandilla?)*
Karen:	No, no. Well, there are a couple that sometimes hang out with us who have colors but we are not into gangs. I got into a couple of fights because I got disrespected, that's all. *(No, no. Bueno, hay algunos que ocasionalmente comparten con nosotros que llevan colores pero nosotros no estamos en pandillas. Me metí en unas cuantas peleas porque me faltaron el respeto, eso es todo.)*
SAP*(PAS)*:	I see. Have any friends or relatives told you that you are drinking or using drugs too much? *(Ya veo. ¿Algunas amistades o familiares te han dicho que estás bebiendo o usando drogas demasiado?)*
Karen:	Oh yeah. Melinda and a couple of kids from school and some of my cousins. Of course, my parents are always on my case but they really don't know how much I drink and do drugs. They just guess it. *(O sí. Melinda y un par de muchachos y algunos de mis primos. Claro está, mis padres están siempre encima de mí, pero en realidad ellos no sabes cuánto bebo y uso drogas. Ellos solo lo suponen.)*
SAP*(PAS)*:	Do you think that your use of drugs and alcohol has caused you trouble? *(¿Piensas que tu uso de drogas y alcohol te ha traído problemas?)*
Karen:	I don't know. I guess so. *(No sé. Supongo que sí.)*
SAP*(PAS)*:	In what way? *(¿En qué manera?)*
Karen:	I guess my temper is worse, and so are my grades and the fighting with my parents. *(Supongo que mi temperamento está peor, y también mis calificaciones y las peleas con mis padres.)*
SAP*(PAS)*:	Have you ever been arrested? *(¿Has sido alguna vez arrestada?)*
Karen:	No, but the cops have stopped me a couple of times and frisked me. *(No, pero los policías me han detenido un par de veces y me han registrado.)*
SAP*(PAS)*:	I guess that none of this happened before you started smoking and drinking. Is that correct? *(Supongo que nada de esto ocurrió antes de que empezaras a fumar y beber. ¿Correcto?)*
Karen:	Yeah. *(Sí.)*
SAP*(PAS)*:	In general, why do you smoke and drink? *(En general, ¿por qué fumas y bebes?)*

Karen:	At first, I did it because my boyfriend gave me a little and I liked it. But now, it helps me deal with all the crap and pressure. *(Al principio, lo hice porque mi novio me dio un poco y me gustó. Pero ahora, esto me ayuda a lidiar con toda la basura y la presión.)*
SAP*(PAS)*:	So it helps you cope with your emotions and thoughts, and with family, social, and academic issues. *(Entonces te ayuda a lidiar con tus emociones y pensamientos, y con asuntos familiares, sociales, y académicos.)*
Karen:	I guess so. *(Supongo que sí.)*
SAP*(PAS)*:	Have you ever heard the word "addiction"? *(¿Has escuchado la palabra "adicción"?)*
Karen:	I'm not a junkie! *(¡Yo no soy una drogadicta!)*
SAP*(PAS)*:	No, I didn't say junkie, I only mentioned the word "addiction." *(No, yo no dije drogadicta, yo solo mencioné la palabra "adicción.")*
Karen:	It's the same thing. *(Es lo mismo).*
SAP*(PAS)*:	Are you concerned about how others see you? *(¿Estás preocupada de cómo te ven los demás?)*
Karen:	I don't care. *(A mí no me importa).*
SAP*(PAS)*:	You say you are not concerned, yet you felt somewhat angry when the word "addiction" was mentioned. *(Dices que no estás preocupada, sin embargo te sentiste un tanto enojada cuando la palabra "adicción" fue mencionada.)*
Karen:	So what's your point? *(Y ¿cuál es su punto?)*
SAP*(PAS)*:	My point is that you need help. Sometimes a substance starts taking control of our lives without hardly being noticed. And in this case, these substances are taking the best out of Karen's life. You are a young, beautiful, and intelligent woman who deserves much better. Fortunately, you have a lot of people who care about you and want the best for you. And, as I said before, I will help you navigate this crisis and provide the best strategies for success. *(Mi punto es que tú necesitas ayuda. A veces una sustancia comienza a tomar control de nuestras vidas sin apenas ser percibida. Y en este caso, estas sustancias están tomando lo mejor de la vida de Karen. Tú eres una mujer joven, hermosa e inteligente que se merece algo mucho mejor. Afortunadamente, tú tienes mucha gente que se preocupan por ti y desean lo mejor para ti. Y, como dije anteriormente, yo voy a ayudarte a manejar esta crisis y proveerte las mejores estrategias para triunfar.)*
Karen:	[Silence accompanied by intense sobbing.] *([Silencio acompañado por sollozos intensos.])*

Frases generales de planificación de tratamiento	General phrases for planning treatment
Usted tendrá que completar la lista diaria de tareas de la agencia que se encuentran escritas en el tablón de edictos.	You will need to complete the daily list of tasks assigned by the agency that are posted on the bulletin board.
Usted tendrá que asistir a todas las sesiones de grupo y estar presente con 5 a 10 minutos de anticipación.	You will need to attend all scheduled group sessions and be there 5 to 10 minutes before they start.
Usted se le asignará un compañero por un periodo de dos semanas. Luego, usted sirvirá de compañero a nuevos clientes.	You will have a "buddy" assigned to you for two weeks. Later on, you will serve as a "buddy" to new clients.
Será su responsabilidad de leer el manual de clientes de la agencia y de familiarizarse con las rutinas diarias.	It will be your responsibility to read the agency's client handbook and to familiarize yourself with daily routines.
Escriba en orden de importancia siete cosas (personas, lugares, situaciones, etc.) que le ocasionan más dificultad para manejarlo.	Write down in order of importance seven things (people, places, situations, etc.) that are most difficult for you to handle.
Escriba los temores y preocupaciones que le mantienen estancado en su presente situación.	Write down the fears and concerns that are keeping you stuck in your current situation.
Haga una lista de todas las cosas que le mantienen preocupado fuera de la agencia de tratamiento.	Make a list of all the things that worry you outside the treatment agency.
Provea ejemplos en los que el negar su situación y el culpar a otros por sus acciones han afectado su responsabilidad personal.	Give examples of how denying your situation and blaming others for your actions have affected your personal responsibility.
Haga una lista de las situaciones de alto riesgo que lo ponen en peligro cuando usted consume alcohol o drogas.	List some high-risk situations that put you in danger when you consume alcohol or drugs.
Haga una lista de miembros de su familia y amistades que no abusan del alcohol o drogas, y que puedan ser de buena influencia para usted.	Make a list of family members and friends who do not abuse alcohol or drugs, and who can be a good influence for you.

¿Cuáles son sus metas durante su estadía en la agencia?	What are your goals during your stay at the agency?
¿Cómo espera usted mantenerse sobrio luego de su salida del programa de tratamiento?	How do you expect to keep yourself sober once you leave the treatment program?
Haga una lista de estrategias para obtener el éxito y su autocontrol.	List your strategies for success and self-control.
¿Cómo manejaría usted una situación de alto riesgo en la cual usted se encuentra estresado y al borde de consumir alcohol o drogas?	How would you handle a high-risk situation in which you find yourself stressed out and about to consume alcohol or drugs?

Changing Your Life by Altering Your Lifestyle

One of the key aspects of defeating a substance abuse issue or an addiction is to alter the daily routines and activities related to using the drugs. This is a challenging and critical aspect because clients must shift their outlook on life and all the things that were considered normal and appropriate. Substituting unhealthy pleasurable activities for healthy ones, and redefining the terms "relaxation" and "fun" are of utmost importance for chemically dependent individuals. The following sections provide a combination of strategies for how to slowly but steadily add elements to the creation of a healthy lifestyle, develop problem-solving skills, and improve social skills.

Lista de actividades placenteras y gratificantes	List of enjoyable and gratifying activities
Comer helado con amigos o seres queridos	Eating ice cream with friends or loved ones
Lavar su camioneta o automóvil	Washing your truck or car
Viajar dentro y fuera del país	Traveling in and out of the country
Salir los fines de semana	Weekend getaways
Deportes acuáticos	Water sports
Proyectos de tejidos (costura)	Sewing projects
Coleccionar artículos	Collecting things
Plantar y jardinería	Planting and gardening
Montar bicicleta en cualquier momento	Bicycling at any time
Patinar	Skating

Reparar o restaurar antiguedades	Repairing and restoring antiques
Hacerse miembro de la biblioteca pública local	Becoming a member of the local public library
Tener relaciones íntimas con su pareja amada	Having intimate relations with a loved partner
Compartir su tiempo con sus seres queridos	Sharing your time with loved ones
Invitar amistades para compartir té, café, desayuno, almuerzo, o cena	Inviting friends over for tea, coffee, breakfast, lunch, or dinner
Tejer y coser	Knitting and sewing
Escuchar música relajante	Listening to relaxing music
Organizar y limpiar su casa	Organizing and cleaning your house
Ir al parque, la playa, o un espacio abierto con tu perro	Going to the park, the beach, or an open space with your dog
Caminar descalzo en la grama o en la playa	Walking barefoot on the grass or the beach
Leer historias cortas, novelas, biografías, o el periódico	Reading short stories, novels, biographies, or the newspaper
Ayudar a un amigo o alguien en necesidad	Helping a friend or someone in need
Levantarse temprano para disfrutar del amanecer	Waking up early to enjoy the sunrise
Tomar el tiempo para disfrutar la fragancia de las flores y plantas en la primavera	Taking the time to enjoy the fragrance of flowers and plants in the spring
Asistir a servicios religiosos y experimentar la presencia de Dios	Attending religious services and experiencing the presence of God
Disfrutar el estar contigo mismo/a y estar en paz consigo mismo/a	Enjoying being by yourself and being at peace with yourself
Ir al cine solo/a o con amigos/as	Going to the movies alone or with friends
Hablar por teléfono con un(a) amigo/a	Talking to a friend on the phone
Salir a comer (con o sin planes previos)	Going out to eat (either planned or unplanned)
Hacerse miembro de un gimnasio y tomar clases de levantamiento de pesas, yoga, o ejercicios aeróbicos	Joining a health club and taking weight training, yoga, or aerobic exercise classes
Presenciar eventos deportivos en vivo	Watching live sport events
Ir a la ciudad o los suburbios	Going to the city or the suburbs

Crear un plan de mejoramiento para su salud en general	Creating a plan to improve your overall health
Disfrutar de la vista escénica mientras manejas, montas bicicleta, o corres	Enjoying the scenery while driving, riding your bike, or running
Pescar en un lugar tranquilo	Fishing in a peaceful place
Preparar una comida especial	Fixing a special meal
Asistir a servicios religiosos frecuentemente	Attending religious services frequently
Reírte de ti mismo/a	Laughing at yourself
Sonreír varias veces durante el día	Smiling several times a day
Acostarse en la grama o en la arena	Lying down on some grass or sand
Tener una buena conversación con su esposo/a	Having a good conversation with your spouse
Disfrutar del campo en tu día libre	Enjoying the countryside during your day off
Practicar deportes	Playing sports
Planificar de antemano actividades únicamente para usted	Planning activities that are just for you
Recompensarte a ti mismo/a con un buen regalo	Treating yourself with a good gift
Hacer proyectos de arte para divertirse	Doing art projects for fun
Decorar un rincón especial de su casa	Decorating a special corner of your house
Asistir a una conferencia auspiciada por la universidad, colegio de la comunidad, o biblioteca local	Attending a lecture at your local university, community college, or library
Meditar en un lugar tranquilo	Meditating in a quiet place
Acampar o estar al aire libre	Camping or being outdoors
Pensar positivamente en torno al futuro	Thinking positively about the future
Jugar juegos de mesa	Playing board games
Trabajar en rompecabezas	Working on puzzles
Tomar un baño caliente con una música agradable de fondo	Taking a hot bath with nice music in the background
Bailar con o sin compañía	Dancing with or without company
Tomar recesos y siestas	Taking breaks and naps
Trabajar manualidades por diversión	Working on crafts for fun
Salir en una cita con una persona especial	Going on a date with a special person

Jugar con mascotas y disfrutar de su energía	Playing with pets and enjoying their energy
Visitar familiares que no ha visto en largo tiempo	Visiting relatives that you have not seen in a while
Ser parte de un comité comunitario	Being part of a community committee
Sentarse bajo el sol mientras está solo/a	Sitting in the sun while you are alone
Escuchar algún programa de radio interesante	Listening to an interesting radio programme
Cantar para sí mismo/a	Singing to yourself
Leer autobiografías de autores/aslatinos/hispanos que han causado un impacto en la comunidad o país	Reading autobiographies of Latino/Hispanic authors who have made an impact in the community or country
Conversar con líderes latinos/hispanos exitosos	Talking to successful Latino/Hispanic leaders

Destrezas sociales (Social Skills)

There are many types of behaviors resulting from the use of drink or drugs that can produce adverse reactions in other people. As people are turned off by these "unusual" or "unexpected" behaviors, an increasing sense of isolation is created around a person who drinks or uses drugs. The following is a list of poor social skills that should be avoided.

Destrezas sociales pobres	**Poor social skills**
Señalar lo negativo siempre	Always pointing out the negative
Expresar su propia lastima a otros/as	Expressing self-pity to others
Demostrar gestos de nerviosismo frente a otros/as	Showing nervous gestures in front of others
Verse enojado/a todo el tiempo	Looking angry all the time
No sonreír a otros	Not smiling at others
Hacer caso omiso de las personas cuando se le acercan	Ignoring people when they approach you
Evitar contacto visual durante las conversaciones	Avoiding eye contact during conversations
No demostrar interés por las vidas de otros/as	Not showing interest in the lives of others

Evitar conversaciones	Avoiding conversations
Pobres hábitos de higiene	Poor hygiene habits
Quejas constantes sobre otros/as, situaciones, y la vida en general	Constant complaining about others, situations, and life in general
Usar auto revelación cuando no es apropiado	Using self-disclosure when not appropriate
Siempre quejándose de su mala suerte y mala fortuna en la vida	Always complaining about your bad luck and misfortune in life

In order to promote better interpersonal relationships with people at work, school, religious organizations, and in society in general, clients must demonstrate a conscious effort to monitor their daily social skills. The more positive and engaging their social skills are, the more positive feedback they will receive from those close to them. The following is a list of positive social skills that engage people.

Destrezas sociales positivas	**Positive social skills**
Buenos hábitos de aseo personal	Good personal hygiene habits
Sonreír a otros	Smiling at others
Señalar lo positivo acerca de las cosas	Pointing out the positive side of things
Expresar una preocupación genuina a cerca de los asuntos de otras personas	Expressing a genuine concern for other people's issues
Utilizar el nombre de las personas y darle el valor por quienes son	Using people's names in conversation and valuing them for who they are
Conversar acerca de cosas placenteras y gratificantes	Talking about enjoyable and satisfying things
Cooperar y ayudar a otros con actividades	Cooperating and helping others with activities
Decirle a otras personas cosas positivas de ellos mismos	Telling other people positive things about themselves
Escuchar con respeto y paciencia cuando otros le hablan	Listening with respect and patience when others talk to you
Usar el tacto adecuado para demostrar interés genuino	Using appropriate tact to demonstrate genuine interest
Demostrar agradecimiento por lo que otros hacen por usted	Showing appreciation for what others do for you
Ser asertivo pero respetuoso	Being assertive but respectful

Destrezas de resolución de problemas (Problem-Solving Skills)

The following list provides basic and general steps for the development of appropriate problem-solving skills.

Desarrollando destrezas de resolución de problemas	Developing problem-solving skills
¿Cuál es el problema al cual usted se está enfrentando?	What is the problem that you are facing?
Defina el problema con especificidad y detalles.	Define the problem clearly and in detail.
¿Cuáles son las metas que quiere alcanzar?	What goals do you want to accomplish?
¿Son estas metas manejables y realistas?	Are these goals manageable and realistic?
A parte de usted, ¿quién y que más se van a beneficiar de los logros de estas metas?	Apart from you, who and what else would benefit from the accomplishment of these goals?
¿Cuáles son todas las alternativas que tiene?	What are all the alternatives that you have?
Haga una lista de todas las alternativas a mano aunque al principio parezcan inalcanzables.	Make a list of all the alternatives at hand, even if some of them initially seem far-fetched.
Estudie todas las alternativas y sus consecuencias.	Study all the alternatives and their consequences.
Elimine las alternativas que pueden traer consecuencias negativas.	Eliminate the alternatives that may have negative consequences.
Coloque en orden jerárquico sus mejores alternativas y en orden de importancia.	Rank your best alternatives in order of importance.
Ejecute estas acciones.	Carry out these actions.
Evalúe los efectos y posibles consecuencias de sus actos.	Evaluate the effects and possible consequences of your actions.
¡Celebre y esté orgulloso/a de tomar sus propias decisiones!	Celebrate and be proud of making your own decisions!

7 Developing Spanish Bilingual Materials and Techniques on How to Work with an Interpreter

The Importance of Developing Spanish Materials

Producing materials in Spanish should be part of a comprehensive plan of bilingual interventions in any mental health agency or school. These materials will complement your newly acquired Spanish skills and send a message that you and your agency are attuned with the bilingual and cultural needs of your clients. Although translation may seem trivial and straightforward to many people, it is a very technical competence that very few people can do with a high degree of accuracy. For instance, I have been into many hospitals, schools, and governmental and social agencies that have the best of intentions in having Spanish translations of several brochures, posters, and handouts. However, to my surprise, many of these documents are plagued with grammatical mistakes, syntax errors, and awkward words because they have been forcefully translated from English into Spanish. Observe that these inaccurate translations can lead to incorrect medical and counseling follow-ups, faulty legal advice, and missed career or job opportunities.

Why Should Your Agency or School Have Materials in Spanish?

There are several reasons for you to have materials in Spanish, but ultimately the most important rationale of all is that your clients will benefit in the long run from messages that are clear and comprehensible. Other reasons are:

1. It can benefit specific sectors of the population such as recent immigrants, field or farm workers, and refugees. In this way some materials can be specifically tailored to their unique cultural and linguistic needs.
2. The assurance that the content is fully understood by your clients and you can be certain that they are in compliance with any legal, state, or federal mandates.
3. It will set an example for other mental health agencies, offices or schools to follow and will increase your reputation as a culturally and linguistically sensitive counselor and agency.

Bilingual Materials: Suggested Recommendations

The following are a set of standards that may help you to generate specific agency or school policies relative to the use of bilingual materials.

1. Establish specific guidelines and procedures relative to the use of foreign-language materials, which should include the need for professional translators. Policies should be written in a way that is sensitive to the average reading level of the clients, and prior to distributing the materials or having them on display for the general public, you should verify that they have been proofread.

2. If the translation project seems to be too onerous and costly, consult and collaborate with other agencies or colleagues who may be engaged in similar projects, in order to minimize costs and time.

3. Do not reinvent the wheel! Consult with other schools, and private and public mental health agencies to determine what materials are already available and easy to reproduce; this will save you time and resources. Verify if the materials are subject to copyright restrictions and obtain the necessary permissions for their reproduction or alteration.

4. Avoid computerized translation programs! Although these are handy tools for non-professional activities, these are not accurate and have many region-specific words that may not mean the same to every Spanish-speaking client. For example, the word *child* can be translated differently in many countries if generic or standard Spanish is not used. Let's say, in Argentina is *pibe*, in Costa Rica is *guagua*, in Venezuela is *chamo*, in Spain *chaval*, and in Mexico *menudo*. The standard word for child is *niño* (masculine) or *niña* (feminine).

5. Try to provide both Spanish and English versions in one document whenever possible. Keep in mind that you may have partially bilingual clients who could benefit from both versions.

6. Once the materials have been translated, either do a back-translation by sending it to another translator to corroborate that the content is consistent or send it to other professional native speakers for feedback and suggestions.

7. Test the materials by consulting a small focus group of clients to see if they are easy to read and comprehend.

8. Like any other materials, Spanish documents need to be updated frequently to make sure that their contents are up-to-date with regard to general information, names of employees and contacts, addresses, phone numbers, changes in the law relative to immigration, and the latest techniques in the counseling field.

Employing Fully Bilingual Specialists for Your Agency or School

For the most part, schools have special provisions to assess the level of bilingual proficiency among teaching and administrative staff. There are specific batteries of tests in which written, oral, and comprehensive language proficiency are measured, and certifications such as Bilingual Specialist and ESL Instructor are issued by the state department of education. These established mechanisms simplify the process of hiring potential school counselors and school psychologists who are bilingual (these, by the way, are in short supply in the field!). However, if you are in a mental health agency that is seeking to enhance its counseling staff by either adding a bilingual interpreter-translator and/or a bilingual counselor, then you will have to devise your own evaluation mechanisms to determine a person's level of Spanish proficiency. Remember that *being a native speaker does not automatically make the person an expert in oral interpretation and the translation of printed material.* For instance, have you noticed how many native English speakers are unable to write a complete and coherent sentence or articulate their thoughts appropriately? Well, the same principle applies to native Spanish speakers!

There are some national certification agencies that can assist organizations in assessing the qualifications and professional credentials of translators. Agencies like the American Translators Association (ATA) (www.atanet.org) provide certificates to those who are professionally trained in this area, offering rigor to the selection of the most competitive applicants. Some public agencies such as school districts and state court systems have devised assessment batteries to evaluate the level of proficiency of translators and interpreters, and also have regulatory mechanisms to assist mental health agencies with the verification process of those who are qualified to work in this field. If you run your own mental health agency or perhaps your supervisors have been thinking about consulting a bilingual expert to translate or create new Spanish documents or maybe to work as a part-time interpreter, the following are suggestions that can simplify this process.

Qualifications for Spanish Bilingual Interpreters and Translators

If you or your mental health agency want to save some capital, there is always the option of hiring volunteers to provide translation and interpretation services. If you choose the volunteer route, and since volunteers are not bound to a professional code of ethics, you should exercise caution when using their services. Just as for any other position, a criminal background check is advisable, because even though they will not be providing direct counseling services, they will have access to written information and confidential conversations that take place in therapy sessions. Nowadays, the criminal background check is simple and you can access information easily by using internet services such as www.intelius.com, in which the profile of the individual is provided for a fee.

From a professional standpoint, and according to the Department of Health and Human Services of the State of North Carolina (1998), the following recommended qualifications should be taken into consideration when hiring a paid or volunteer bilingual translator/interpreter either temporarily or full time:

1. A college degree or a substantial amount of credit hours with a high level of fluency in writing and speaking both English and Spanish.

2. A demonstrated ability to write in Spanish at a reading level appropriate to intended target audiences.
3. Considerable knowledge of the subject area, vocabulary, and technical terms, and experience in producing materials in the area.
4. Knowledge of the idiomatic language differences among Spanish-speaking countries.
5. Technical skills related to the development of materials, including computer literacy and copyediting.
6. Familiarity with graphic arts so specialists can work with a graphic artist in ensuring readability and in determining the appropriateness of illustrations, photographs, and other elements.
7. Familiarity with the culture and reading level of the target audience.
8. An equivalent combination of education and experience (p.38).

Hiring a potential employee, either temporarily or permanently, to join a mental health agency is always challenging. In this field, whether the bilingual specialist is hired only to complete a translation project (i.e. a manual, form, or pamphlet) or to provide ongoing interpretation services during family, group, or individual counseling services, you must ensure that the best candidate is selected.

In spite of the fact that you may know or have acquired decent Spanish-speaking skills, it is advisable to bring a professional native speaker as part of the search committee to assist you in determining the level of proficiency of the candidate. The following are a series of sample questions that can provide some direction during the interview process of a bilingual specialist:

a) Can you provide a series of sample materials that you have produced for other agencies in Spanish and English?
b) Do you have any film or sound recordings of you providing interpretation services?
c) Can you interpret equally well during individual, group, and family sessions?
d) How would you handle a situation in which you knew the client personally?
e) Are you a native Spanish speaker? If not, how much training and cultural immersion do you have in Spanish? In what Latin American countries have you lived? Did you receive your formal education there? At what level (i.e. K–12, undergraduate, graduate)?
f) Are you affiliated with a professional association such as the American Translators Association (ATA)? Do you have any credentials in the field?
g) What is your method of charging (i.e. per hour, page, word, document)?
h) Do you use any special software?
i) Do you charge extra for proofreading the final manuscript or document?
j) In what area of interpretation and translation have you specialized (i.e. medical, educational, legal, psychological)?
k) Can you provide a rough estimate of the number of interpretation sessions and documents translated during your career?

You can also use the following "in-house" evaluation tools for a more comprehensive overview of the bilingual specialist candidate that you are intending to hire for your school or agency.

1. Set up a mock interview, either a typical intake assessment session in which basic mental health questions are formulated in order to render a DSM-IV-TR multiaxial diagnosis (Axes 1–5) or an average counseling session. You can serve as the counselor and a Spanish speaker can serve as the client, so the prospective bilingual specialist can provide the interpretation service. If informed consent has been provided by the interviewee, audiotape the session if possible. This will give you time to go over it and make an informed decision with the rest of the staff.

2. Generate a series of essay questions in Spanish and allow the candidate a reasonable amount of time to answer them. The questions must be answered by hand, and without access to any books or computers. The main idea is to evaluate the linguistic knowledge of the interviewee without the assistance of electronic dictionaries or computerized translators. Of course, you should ensure that a professional native speaker evaluates the answers. The following are a sample of some potential questions that could be included:

    a. En experiencias anteriores, ¿cuáles han sido las mayores dificultades que usted ha enfrentado durante una sesión de consejería mientras usted interpretaba? *(In previous experiences, what have been the biggest challenges that you have faced during a counseling session while you were interpreting?)* _____

    b. ¿Dónde aprendió a hablar español y cuán frecuentemente lo utiliza? *(Where did you learn to speak Spanish and how frequently do you use it?)*

    _____

    c. ¿Qué es lo más que le gusta de ser un intérprete o traductor? ¿Qué es lo menos que le gusta? *(What do you like the most about being an interpreter or translator? What do you like the least?)* _____

    _____

    d. ¿Usted domina otros idiomas? ¿Cuáles? *(Do you have a good command of other languages? Which ones?)* _____

    e. Explique la importancia del bilingüismo en los Estados Unidos. ¿Cuál es su opinión en relación a la educación bilingüe? *(Explain the importance of bilingualism in the United States. What is your opinion on bilingual education?)*_____

    _____

3. Develop your own self-evaluation *Language Proficiency Scale* to compare the scale's scores with your own observations and the performance of the candidate. In other words, sometimes interpreters and translators can have impressive qualifications on a resume and may speak highly about their skills in an interview, but these are not necessarily apparent when tested in a real practical situation. The following is a basic scale that can be used as an example or altered according to your needs and what you are specifically looking for in a candidate for your school or mental health agency:

Scale: Please rate your oral language skills.

Very limited = I have trouble talking with native speakers who have the equivalent of a high school education.

Limited = I may need help or supervision talking with native speakers who have the equivalent of a high school education.

Adequate = I am as fluent as the average native speaker with a high school education.

Good = I am as fluent as any other native speaker who has the equivalent of a college education.

Excellent = I am completely fluent and have a wider vocabulary than most native speakers with the equivalent of a college education.

English Language

Are you an English native speaker? Yes ___ No___

If you answered yes, which US state or other English-speaking country are you from?_____

Please rate your abilities in the following areas of English.

	Very limited	Limited	Adequate	Good	Excellent
Speaking					
Writing					
Vocabulary					
Knowledge of idioms and regionalisms					

Spanish Language

Are you a Spanish native speaker? Yes ___ No ___
If you answered yes, which Latin American country, US state, or Spanish region are you from? _____

Please rate your abilities in the following areas of Spanish.

	Very limited	Limited	Adequate	Good	Excellent
Speaking					
Writing					
Vocabulary					
Knowledge of idioms and regionalisms					

Establishing Rules for the Interpretation Process

Interpreters are not mental health or educational professionals; for this reason, you will have to develop a plan to establish the rules of the therapeutic process. Even for short intake and follow-up evaluations or counseling sessions, it is of extreme importance to communicate frequently with the interpreter to ensure the success of the process. The following are some general guidelines that can assist you when working with an interpreter to ensure a degree of success.

1. Use generic language without regionalisms

Broadcasted Spanish and generic English are best when communicating with an interpreter and a client. If as a professional mental health professional you utilize extremely technical language, your interpreter will be obligated to improvise and come up with equivalent terminology that will not necessarily convey the essence of your message. Your interpreter is highly advised to avoid regionalism-free dialects that could be misinterpreted by your client. The idea is to make the conversation as clear as possible without unnecessary clarifications and reinterpretations that consume time and are conducive to misunderstandings.

2. Clarify the role of the interpreter as a communicator of messages, rather than a decision-maker

The language and cultural compatibility between the interpreter and the client are elements that could potentially inadvertently derail the communication between you and your client. The interpreter (especially if he/she is not a certified interpreter) must be informed that he/she must not make decisions for you or the client, and should not answer questions for the client assuming that they are accurate. For instance, let's say that one of the questions is: Do you smoke? Perhaps the interpreter assumes that the client is not a smoker based on a previous comment and says "no" without even consulting the client. This is unacceptable because the job of the interpreter is to accurately relay all communications to and from the client and mental health professional, without adding or omitting anything.

3. Prevent side conversations between the client and interpreter.

The independent and unique roles of the mental health professional or school counselor must be clarified from the beginning. Professional interpreters should be clear about their roles and the delimitations of their expertise, but occasionally, if the individual is an in-house interpreter who happens to know the language and the culture but is not a certified national interpreter, then it is critical to clarify his/her position in the therapeutic process. The interpreter must not have side conversations, either before or after any intervention with the client. Additional or side conversations in the absence of the mental health professional erode the trust of the therapeutic relationship and send a mixed signal to the client as to who has the expertise in the situation.

4. Allow the client to take the initiative during the session.

Typically, the mental health professional prompts the client to converse and share current issues or bring relevant information to the therapeutic process. It is not the role of the interpreter to initiate a conversation or prompt the client to talk. Always allow the client to take the initiative, as in a traditional therapy session without an interpreter.

5. Sequential versus concurrent mode of translation.

The *concurrent mode of translation* is based on maintaining the flow of the conversation without interruptions to either the mental health professional or the client. This is an extremely difficult way of interpreting, which is commonly used during United Nations sessions by highly trained experts with an excellent command of both languages and interpreting techniques. This is not recommended in a mental health or school counseling context, as too many details are commonly ignored or inadvertently missed; also, it creates confusion and seems hectic. In contrast, the *sequential mode of translation* consists first in a comment or question being made by the mental health professional, then its translation by the interpreter, then the response of the client, and finally the translation of this response back to the mental health professional by the interpreter. Although the sequential mode is slower than the concurrent mode of translation, it is more effective and accurate with respect to content delivery, and also prevents the mental health professional of rendering inaccurate diagnoses or making misinformed decisions.

6. Be cognizant of the cultural context and ask for occasional input from the interpreter.

Although it is preferred to consult with the interpreter before and after a session, occasionally it is necessary to make a quick clarification about a word or a concept from a cultural framework in order to keep the conversation going. Avoid having prolonged conversations with the interpreter in the presence of the client in order to prevent misunderstandings and sending the message that you are talking about the client "behind his/her back" so to speak.

7. Inform the client with respect to the interpretation process, and the professional and ethical standards expected.
The client must be informed about the role of the interpreter and the limitations of this linguistic professional. The client must be educated that the interpreter is bound to the same principles of confidentiality and privacy with respect to all communications during the sessions. It is critical to indicate that the role of the interpreter is simply to serve as a communication channel between the mental health professional and the client. Also, depending on the situation, the interpreter will serve as cultural buffer in order to smooth the communication between the mental health professional and the client.

8. Time and pace.
Maintaining a measured pace during counseling sessions is a key element for promoting therapeutic change and growth. The same principle applies to sessions in which an interpreter is involved, although it is highly advised that these counseling interventions should be concise and to the point. Long and convoluted interventions are difficult to translate and can provoke confusion; points may be missed, and counseling sessions can slow down too much. Bear in mind that the duration of a counseling session with an interpreter will be approximately double that of a traditional counseling session, because your comments and questions and the client's responses must all be repeated. In sum, without taking away any spontaneity from the counseling sessions and without eliminating the power of the here-and-now, it is advisable for the mental health professional to have a clear agenda and predefined goals prior to the beginning of each session in which an interpreter will be present, in order to maximize the use of time in that session.

9. Meet with the interpreter before and after every session.
Giving some background about the client to the interpreter prior to the counseling session provides a framework of reference and helps both of you to strategize relative to potential dynamics. After the end of every session, the mental health professional should consult with the interpreter to see if there are some cultural elements that must be considered with respect to the diagnosis and progress notes.

Interpreting Techniques

There are various techniques and styles of interpretation; therefore, the interpreter and counselor must confer and find out what works best and what will benefit the clients the most.

Physical Set-Up

The physical set-up sets the atmosphere for the processes and dynamics to be followed and sends a non-verbal message relative to the establishment of the communication channels and the flow of information. You must arrange the physical set-up in advance, before the beginning of a session. Typically, and just like in a traditional counseling session, you will come out, greet the client in the waiting area, and invite him or her to your office. In the office, the interpreter will be waiting for the arrival of you and the client. Upon arrival in the office, you will lead the client to the designated seating area. Keep in mind that the initial contact must be made by you and not the interpreter. This sends the message that you are facilitating the counseling process, providing the information, and will ultimately be rendering a diagnosis (if needed). Hopefully, your initial contract of confidentiality will have a statement relative to the utilization of interpreting services during the counseling sessions, so the presence of the interpreter in the office should not be a surprise to your client. However, you can also remind the client about the presence of the interpreter in the office immediately after the formal greetings in the reception area. For example:

Counselor: Buenos dias, Sr. García. Yo soy el Sr. Patrick, su consejero profesional. En la oficina se encuentra la Sra. Ferré, la cual servirá de intérprete durante nuestra sesión. (*Good morning, Mr. García. I am Mr. Patrick, your professional counselor. In the office is Ms. Ferré, who will be serving as an interpreter during our session.*)

Positioning the Interpreter and the Client

Although there are many types of settings, the one that tends to work best according to my experience is what I call the *triangle arrangement.* In essence, the client is positioned at the tip of the triangle and the counselor and interpreter are sitting side by side at the base of the triangle both facing the client. The client will have complete visual access to both (counselor and interpreter), which will prevent the client from looking to the side and feeling distracted during the conversations (see Figure 7.1 below). It is also encouraged that you look at the *reader's companion website's interpretation session* to see how the dynamics of interpretation are managed. The interpretation session will provide you with an illustration as to how an

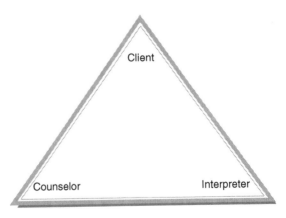

Figure 7.1 Triangle arrangement

English-monolingual mental health professional arranges the physical set-up and manages the pace of the therapeutic session. Listen carefully to the translation and follow the strategy of the professional in your own sessions.

The client should be educated about the flow of the communication and instructed that he/she should communicate normally without saying: "Tell the counselor that ..." as this would otherwise delay communication and could be somewhat awkward and convoluted. Remember that the interpreter should also be instructed to repeat exactly what you and the client are saying without any redundant phrases, as for instance, "The client told me to tell you that ..." Being repetitive by reiterating who said what simply interrupts the translation process.

Ethical Issues

During traditional counseling sessions between clients and mental health professionals who share the same gender, sexual orientation, ethnicity, race, and socioeconomic status, differences tend to be minimized. However, even among so-called homogeneous interactions, differences in perception and interpretation abound and a myriad of potential ethical issues arise. If to the aforementioned variables the elements of language and ethnic differences are added, the number of ethical issues is multiplied.

Avoid Using Family Members as Interpreters (Especially Children)

Family members cannot assure accuracy, confidentiality, or objectivity in any therapeutic process. The utilization of children as interpreters is contraindicated because they do not have the knowledge or emotional maturity to process complex human issues that they have not experienced themselves from a human development standpoint. Moreover, children can be traumatized by vicarious experiences of family members, which can severe their relationships and ultimately damage their emotional and psychological stability. Furthermore, the use of minors as renderers of services is not only unethical but illegal, because they lack the professional training and the maturity to be able to maintain the confidentiality and privacy of the client: in this case, a family member. As usual, when in doubt, it is better to consult with other colleagues who have used interpreting services in the past and can advise on the best practices possible, especially when working with children (Lopez, 2002).

Modulate the Volume of Your Voice

Speaking louder does not help a client with limited English proficiency understand better; on the contrary, it may actually provoke intimidation or could be interpreted as being rude. In contrast, using a "therapeutic" or soft voice encourages the client to be at ease and to disclose information. The best recommended technique is to imagine that your client can understand you completely and is following you through the conversation. Remember that you would not raise your voice in therapy to one of your English-speaking clients.

Consider Gender as a Cultural Element

Within the Latino/Hispanic community, gender differences are typically delineated, and depending on the level of cultural assimilation or the number of years in the new host country, it may be likely that your client will be more open to be counseled by someone of the same gender. For instance, let's imagine that you are a male counselor with expertise in sexual education and couples relationships and you were referred a Latino/Hispanic male client who was experiencing erectile dysfunction issues. To begin with, the revelation and acceptance of having a sexual deficiency issue is difficult in itself for most males, and it is perhaps more difficult for Latino/Hispanic male clients, as sexual vigor is correlated with being a man (Mirandé, 1997). This is consistent with the ideas of machismo and strength. Imagine a scenario in which you have in your office a female interpreter to assist you with the sessions. Can you imagine the reactions of your Latino/Hispanic male client? Do you honestly believe that he will disclose or talk about any intimate issues in front of a female interpreter? Do you believe that he will feel offended?

Now, reverse the case and picture a female counselor with expertise in sexuality and trauma who is referred a female Latin a client. Envision the reaction and surprise of the client when she sees a male interpreter in the office. Do you believe that she will be comfortable disclosing her detailed story about being raped or sexually molested? Do you believe that she will be relaxed mentioning her sexual issues with her current partner as a result of this incident?

Because there is a likelihood that clients will be challenged by the presence of someone of the opposite sex as an interpreter, you will have to exercise prudence when selecting the best match based on the situation at hand.

Using Interpreters from the Community

Coincidences abound whenever human beings interact. For instance, it is not unusual that a client who comes to your agency seeking counseling services is an acquaintance of yours. Normally, we would refer these clients to another colleague in order to provide the best services for them, as we are looking to promote objectivity in the counseling process; this also serves as a mechanism to preserve the ties of friendship. Likewise, friends or even vague acquaintances should not provide interpreting services. This will include people who belong to the same church, sports club, neighborhood, or social organization. This will prevent awkward dynamics in the counseling session or outside in the community.

Consider the Ethnicity and Dialect of the Client with Limited English Proficiency when Selecting an Interpreter

It is not uncommon in certain sectors of the Latino/Hispanic population to be originally from remote Latin American regions in which Spanish is not the primary language. For instance, there are regions in Guatemala, Peru, and Bolivia in which Spanish is only used by indigenous populations when in contact with individuals from larger towns or cities. As a result, the assumption that all Latino/Hispanic clients have full mastery of the Spanish language is not accurate. Consequently, the interpreter should have some background about the client's language or dialect prior to engaging in the counseling process.

Using Non-Professional Staff in Schools as Interpreters

There are times when out of necessity and in the spur of the moment, a school counsel or might be tempted to use the non-professional services of any school staff member; but this would bring a series of ethical and legal issues to the equation. For instance, it is likely (although this is a general assumption) that the school gardener, janitor, painter, cafeteria staff member, or handy person will have a limited formal education and no training in interpretation techniques; as a result, the quality of their services will be questionable. Also, since this staff member would not be bound to a code of ethics pertaining to educators, school counselors, social workers and psychologists, issues of confidentiality and privacy would be a strong concern. It is very possible that this staff member might be an active member of the local church, a community organization, or society in general. Therefore, exposing intimate aspects of the lives of school children and their parents should be an important consideration, and can be avoided by using the services of professionally trained interpreters.

Non-Verbal Communication: The "Silent" Cross-Cultural Elements to be Considered in Counseling

Just like any other ethnic group, the Latino/Hispanic community is facing constant transition and reconstruction. For instance, within a generation or two a single family may have immigrated to the U.S. and also migrated from a rural to an urban setting. During this period, families and communities deal with social and economic variations that affect social roles and personal worldviews. Taking these elements into consideration and emphasizing the idea of individual differences and diversity among individuals of Latino/Hispanic descent, there are some areas that should be addressed to enhance your repertoire of cultural tools (Lopez, 2002).

Submission to Authority

In general, as has been mentioned before, traditional Latino/Hispanic families tend to be patriarchal. Overall obedience to the father is expected in a family system that reflects the systemic idea of submitting to local authorities such as school teachers, police officers, military personnel, heads of state, religious figures, and political leaders. Since South and Central America were conquered by southern European countries (Spain and Portugal) and influenced by the stratified structured of the Catholic Church and the authority of the Pope, the Latin American culture absorbed many of the intricate social values from these patriarchal institutions. The concept of submission is viewed as a sign of respect, education, and honor. If these signs of respect and submission are extrapolated to the counseling context, it is expected that Latino/Hispanic clients will tend to be more compliant and less confrontational than average US clients.

The concept of submission in counseling could represent a challenge to the counselor who expects to "empower" a client by providing information or by role-playing scenarios of independent behaviors during therapy sessions. Bear in mind that out of respect and submission, your clients may agree to do and say certain things even if deep inside they are uncomfortable or do not intend to go through with the plan. Similarly, if your clients seem to be somewhat passive and not engaged in the counseling process this should not necessarily be interpreted as resistance or lack of compliance with the treatment. It is likely that your clients are just listening and following the instructions you have given them. For some clients, especially those who lack formal education, the idea of being independent thinkers or being in charge of all decisions is a foreign concept. Not only that, but many clients would expect *consejos* (advice), meaning that you will tell them exactly what, how, and when to do things. A non-directive counseling approach could be more challenging for some clients. Then again, Latino/Hispanic clients with formal and advanced education with a European background have been exposed to different schools of thought and life philosophies, and are as adept at non-directive and personal growth techniques as any mainstream US client.

The Concept of Personal Space

Studies of cross-cultural behaviors among Latin Americans, and more specifically among Latinos/Hispanics in the US, have not been sufficient to be able to make conclusive decisions relative to considerations of space and physical contact during conversations. For instance, Argyle (1988) indicates that Latin Americans make more eye contact, face each other more, and touch more when they speak (p.58). However, these observations are based on certain situations and social contexts, such as interactions with friends, family, when dating, or among married couples (p.60). Based on my personal and professional experiences, there are tremendous intra-ethnic and regional differences among Latin Americans. For instance, individuals from the Caribbean (i.e. Puerto Rico, the Dominican Republic, and Cuba) tend to touch and speak very close to each other. Likewise, some South Americans (i.e. Argentinians, Colombians, and Venezuelans) are very animated, use physical contact to emphasize points in a conversation, and interrupt each other frequently. Again, most of these behaviors are very contextual and it is not unusual among mental health professionals to ask during a conversation with their clients if they can refer to them as *tú,* which is the informal counterpart of *usted.* It is interesting to point out that Americans do the same among themselves when they ask if they can refer to a person by his/her first name and drop the Mr./Mrs./Ms. or professional title. However, among populations with a strong indigenous influence such as Guatemala, Peru, Ecuador, Mexico, and Bolivia, the physical distance and the *formalismo* (formality) are maintained for longer than among other ethnic Latin American groups. Likewise, intense eye contact is not the norm among individuals of indigenous ancestry, unlike for those who have a mixed European background. It is critical to remember that just as Native Indian Americans in the US have suffered territorial displacement and cultural domination, Native Indians in Central and South America have also been victims of genocides, persecution, and discrimination for centuries. Depending on the country of origin and the levels of interethnic admixture, these dynamics will be evident to a greater or lesser degree. Nevertheless, it is expected that most of your Latino/Hispanic clients will maintain a formal spatial distance between themselves and you during counseling sessions, and will keep you at arm's length (at the very least). This is only natural, since they are seeing a professional with technical knowledge and experience, and not a friend or family member.

Modesty, Privacy, Dress, and Appearance

So far you have seen that there can be no cookie-cutter approach when working with Latino/Hispanic people due to the vast intra-ethnic, regional, and national differences among them. The issue of socioeconomic status runs deep in Latin America and is more observable than in the US. The abyss between social classes is deeper in Latin America because in general (although depending on the country), there are small upper and middle classes, and fairly large poor sectors. Unfortunately, the issue of class is also closely linked to race. Individuals from upper-class sectors tend to be the descendants of wealthy European settlers; the middle classes have a combination of all ethnic groups (e.g., Europeans, mestizos), who have worked and studied to ascend the socioeconomic ladder; and it is very likely that individuals of black and Indian descent will be disproportionally represented in the poorest sectors of Latin American societies. It is to be expected that individuals of great economic wealth will have a sense of entitlement and a subtle sense of preeminence, regardless of their country of origin. Conversely, individuals with limited economic means, little or no formal education, and scarce world exposure will have more modest attitudes. Their clothing may be simple or unassuming but you will notice the importance their give to having their clothes clean, ironed, and matching other accessories. This is notable when families go out to dine, or when they attend church services on Sunday or birthday celebrations, or when they meet with a professional. You will notice that jewelry (even if inexpensive) and accessories are of much importance. Being clean and presentable for an occasion is important to Latinos/Hispanics as they attempt to honor the place, the people they are meeting with, and the occasion. It is a demonstration of pride and honor.

Summary Guidelines for Mental Health Professionals, School Counselors, and School Psychologists

Sometimes you may need a quick reference to provide direction to your counseling sessions. The following table provides a list of cultural and social elements, and contrasts the average American Euro/Anglo middle-class perspective with the average Latino/Hispanic perspective.

Cultural/Social Element	Average Euro/Anglo American Middle-Class View	Average Latino/Hispanic View
Gender Interaction	Informal and relaxed.	Formal and somewhat distant until a friendship develops.
Formality of Address	Use informal "you" for all relationships.	Have both a formal (*usted*) and an informal(*tú*) form of "you."
Greetings	A solid handshake.	A gentler handshake, hug, or kiss on the cheek.
Eye Contact	Direct eye contact is a sign of respect, honesty and attention.	Averting one's eyes shows respect for an elder or a person of authority.
Communication Method	Direct communication is preferred (say what you mean and mean what you say).	Indirect communication (if it is upsetting, don't say it. "Yes" can mean "maybe" or even "no" depending on the circumstance).
Time	Time is limited and finite so one must fit one's needs to deadlines and schedules. Future-oriented.	Time is relative, expanding and contracting. There is always time, human needs are more important, deadlines can be changed. Enjoying the here-and-now is very important. Present-oriented.

The Concept of Family	Nuclear family, children encouraged to be independent.	Extended family including neighbors and friends, independence can be viewed as disloyal.
Orientation	Focus on the individual, independence, personal fulfillment.	Focus on core groups, looking out for others, achieving group harmony.
Authority and Social Organization	All people are equal, authority can be challenged.	Power is centralized, should defer to authority.
Control	Individuals have control, problems should be "fixed," change is good.	Individuals have little control over destiny, should adapt to problems, change disrupts harmony.
Learning	Interactive, experiential, draw one's own conclusions.	Instructor guides students in a formal manner, dependent on written materials.
Locus of Control	Internal, we control the environment.	External, environmental conditions exert control over our lives.
Expression of Feelings	Controlled and limited manifestations in public of anger, joy, and sadness.	Less restricted, manifestations of feelings are necessary to show sensitivity.
Spirituality	Existent but not very intrusive in daily life.	Spiritual realm has control over the material world.

References

Abalos, D. T. (2002). *The Latino male: A radical redefinition*. Boulder, CO.: Lynn Rienner.

Akmir, A. (2009). *Los árabes en América Latina: Historia de una emigración*. Madrid: Siglo XXI-Casa Árabe.

Allied Media Hispanic Publication Network (2009). Hispanic marketing and media. Retrieved from http://www.allied-media.com/hispanic%20market/hispanic%20publications.html

Allied Media Hispanic Publication Network (2009). Hispanic television, Latino American media, and Hispanic American Television programs. Retrieved from http://www.allied-media.com/hispanic%20market/hispanic%20tv.html.

American Counseling Association. (2005). What is a school counselor? A resource guide for parents and students. Retrieved from www.counseling.org.

American School Counseling Association. (2010). Career/Roles. Retrieved from http://www.schoolcounselor.org/content.asp?contentid=133.

Araújo, B. & Borrell, L. (2006). Understanding the link between discrimination, mental health outcomes, and life chances among Latinos. *Hispanic Journal of Behavioral Sciences*, 28(2), 245–266.

Argyle, M. (1988), *Bodily communication* (2nd ed). London: Methuen & Co. Ltd.

Baker, S. B. & Gerler, E. R., Jr. (2008). *School counseling for the twenty-first century* (5th ed). Upper Saddle River, NJ: Pearson Education.

Benitez, C. (2007). *Latinization: How Latino culture is transforming the U.S.* New York: Paramount Market Publishing.

Benjamin, T. (2000). A time of reconquest: History, the Maya revival, and the Zapatista rebellion. *The American Historical Review*, 105(2), 417–450.

Benson, S. G., Kanellos, N. & Ryan, B. (Eds). (2002). *UXL Hispanic American Reference Library: Chronology* (2nd ed). Belmont, CA: Gale-Cengage.

Berruecos, L. (1976). *El Compadrazgo en América Latina: Análisis Antropológico de 106 Casos*. México: Instituto Indigenista Interamericano.

Bergad, L. W. (2011). *Latino Data Project*. Retrieved from http://web.gc.cuny.edu/lastudies/latinodataprojectreports/The%20Latino%20Population%20of%20New%20York%20City%202009.pdf.

Bloom, B. S. (1956). *Taxonomy of educational objectives*. Boston, MA: Allyn and Bacon.

Bueno, E. & Ceasar, T. (1998). *Imagination beyond nation: Latin American popular culture*. Pittsburgh, PA: University of Pittsburgh Press.

Campbell, L. (1997). *American Indian languages: The historical linguistics of native America*. Oxford: Oxford University Press.

Cantón Navarro, J. (1998). *History of Cuba.* Havana, Cuba: Si-mar.

Cantón Navarro, J. & Jacomino, J. (1998). *History of Cuba: The challenge of the yoke and the star: Biography of a people.* Havana, Cuba: Si-mar.

Carrera, M. M. (2003). *Imagining identity in New Spain: Race, lineage, and the colonial body in portraiture and casta paintings.* Austin, TX: University of Texas Press.

Castro-Feinberg, R. (2002). *Bilingual education: A reference handbook.* Santa Barbara, CA: ABC CLIO.

Christensen, C. B., Wolfe, E. D. & Ponce de León, L. S. (1981). *Vistas hispánicas: Introducción a la lengua y la cultura.* (2nd ed). Boston, MA: Houghton Mifflin.

Clayton, L. A. (2011). *Bartolomé de las Casas and the conquest of the Americas.* Chichester, UK: Wiley.

Clemmer, R. O. (1995). *Roads in the sky: The Hopi Indians in A century of change.* Boulder, CO: Westview Books.

Cohen, J. S. (2007). DePaul degree puts new focus on Hispanics: Major helps students meet corporate need to reach the diverse Latino marketplace. *Chicago Tribune.* January 7, 2007. Retrieved from: http://articles.chicagotribune.com/2007-01-11/news/0701110090_1_latino-consumers-hispanic-business-fastest-growing-ethnic-group.

Cook, V. J. (1995). Multi-competence and the learning of many languages. *Language, Culture and Curriculum 8*(2), 93–98.

Cook, V. J. (1997). The consequences of bilingualism for cognitive processing. In A. de Groot & J. F. Kroll (Eds.), *Tutorials in bilingualism: Psycholinguistic perspectives* (120–176). New York: Lawrence Erlbaum.

Cook, V. J. (2003). *Effects of the second language on the first.* Clevedon, UK: Multilingual Matters.

Corey, G., Callanan, P. & Schneider-Corey, M. (2010). *Issues and ethics in the helping professions.* Pacific Grove, CA: Brooks/Cole.

Cubano, A. I. (1993). *Un puente entre Mallorca y Puerto Rico: La emigración de Sóller, 1830–1930.* Colombres, Spain: Archivos de Indianos.

Cuny Graduate Center. (2009). *The Latino Ph. D. project.* Retrieved from http://web.gc.cuny.edu/lastudies/docs/The%20Latino%20Ph.D.%20Project,%20CLACLS%20CUNY.pdf.

Davies, E. (2006). Unlocking the secret sounds of language: Life without time or numbers. *The Independent.* May 6, 2006. Retrieved from http://www.independent.co.uk/news/science/unlocking-the-secret-sounds-of-language-life-without-time-or-numbers-477061.html.

Diamond, J. (2005). *Guns, germs, and steel: The fates of human societies.* London: W. W. Norton

Fall Demographics (2010) *Household: Spanish or Hispanic origin or descent.* MRI+ Mediamark Reporter database 2010. Retrieved from http://www.mriplus.com/ (accessed October 3, 2011).

Felsch, S. (2006). *The US Hispanic market.* Retrieved from http://www.ajwwarehousing.com/uploads/mz/0B/mz0BZg7ZBUki4kSkbjvWiQ/Hispanic-Market-Report—Full.pdf.

Ferbel, P. J. (2002). Not everyone who speaks Spanish is from Spain: Taíno survival in the 21st century Dominican Republic. *Kacike: Journal of Caribbean Amerindian History and Anthropology.* Retrieved from http://www.kacike.org/FerbelEnglish.html.

Fernández-Morales, M. J. (2002*). La emigración española a Venezuela.* Madrid, Spain: Universidad Complutense de Madrid.

Forbes (2010). *The world's billionaires.* Retrieved from http://www.forbes.com/lists/2010/10/billionaires-2010_The-Worlds-Billionaires_Rank.html.

Gessler, A. (1998). The language learning center – Spanish. *Hispanic culture capsules*. Roanoke, VA: Gastler Publishing.

Giesbrecht, A. B., Printers, F. & Plata, L. (1995). *Immigrants from Canada between 1926 and 1935 found in Die ersten mennonitschen Einwanderer in Paraguay*. Asunción, Paraguay: Asociación Mennonita del Paraguay.

Gott, R. (2004). *Cuba: A new history*. New Haven, CT: Yale University Press.

Gorenstein, S. (1993). Introduction. In Pollard, H. P. (Ed.), *Taríacuri's legacy: The prehispanic Tarascan state*. Norman, OK: University of Oklahoma Press.

Grube, N. (2006). *Los mayas: Una civilización milenaria*. Potsdam, Germany: Ullmann & Könemann.

Guitar, L. (1998). Cultural genesis: Relationships among Indians, Africans and Spaniards in rural Hispaniola, first half of the sixteenth century. (Doctoral dissertation).

Hakuta, K., Butler, Y. & Witt, D. (2000). How long does it take English learners to attain proficiency? *Policy Report 2001. University of California Linguistic Minority Research Institute*. Retrieved from http://www.standford.edu/-hakuta/Docs/HowLong.pdf.

Hartlyn, J. (1998). *The struggle for democratic politics in the Dominican Republic*. Chapel Hill, NC: The University of North Carolina Press.

Hernández, T. K. (2005). (Speech). *"Discrimination and education in the Latin-America"*. Retrieved from http://www.oas.org/en/media_center/speech.asp?sCodigo=05-0286.

Imai, K. (1997). *Los inmigrantes japoneses en Argentina*. Buenos Aires, Argentina: Instituto Japonés.

Inter-American Dialogues, Inter-American Development Bank, World Bank (2000). *Race and poverty: Interagency consultation on Afro–Latin Americans*. Proceedings of the round-table, held June 19, 2000 in Washington, D.C.

Johnson, C. & Smith, P. (1999). *Africans in America: America's journey through slavery*. New York: Harvest Books.

Jordan Institute for Families (1999). Improve your ability to serve Hispanic families. *Children's Services Practice Notes for North Carolina's Child Welfare Social Workers* 4(1). Retrieved from http://www.practicenotes.org/vol4_no1/improveyourability. htm.

Klich, I. (2006). *Árabes y judíos en Latinoamérica: Historia, representaciones y desafíos*. Buenos Aires, Argentina: Asociación por los Derechos Civiles.

Kochlar, R., Gonzalez-Barrera, A. & Dockerman, D. (2009, May). *Through boom and bust: Minorities, immigrants, and homeownership*. Retrieved from http://pewhispanic.org/ reports/report.php? ReportID=109.

Krashen, S. (1996). *Under attack: The case against bilingual education*. Culver City, CA: Language Education Associates.

Limón, J. E. (1998). *American encounters: Greater Mexico, the United States, and the erotics of culture*. Boston, MA: Beacon Press.

Logan, J. R. (2004). How race counts for Hispanic Americans. *Sage Race Relations Abstracts*, 29(1), 7–19.

Look-lai, W. & Tan, C. B. (2010). *The Chinese in Latin America and the Caribbean*. Berkeley, CA: Brill Publications.

Lopez, E. C. (2002). Best practices in working with school interpreters to deliver psychological services to children and families. In J. Grimes & A. Thomas (Eds.), *Twenty seven best practices in school psychology* (pp. 1419–1532). Washington, DC: National Association of School Psychologists.

Lopez, M. H. & Dockterman, D. (2011). *U.S. Hispanic country of origin counts for nation: Top 30 metropolitan areas.* Retrieved from http://pewhispanic.org/reports/report. php?ReportID=142.

Lopez, M. H. & Velasco, G. (2011). *A demographic portrait of Puerto Ricans.* Retrieved from http://pewhispanic.org/reports/report.php?ReportID=143.

Marin, G., Sabogal, F., Vanoss-Marin, B., Otero-Sabogal, R. & Perez-Stable, E. J. (1987). Development of a short acculturation scale for Hispanics. *Hispanic Journal of Behavioral Sciences, 9*(2), 183–205.

Mayo, Y. (1997). Machismo, fatherhood, and the Latino family: Understanding the concept. *Journal of Multicultural Social Work, 5*(12), 49–61.

Mirandé, A. (1997). *Hombres y machos: Masculinity and Latino culture.* Boulder, CO: Westview Press.

Mito, Y. (2007). *Corporate culture as strong driving force for punctuality: Another 'just in time'.* Retrieved from hitachi-rail.com.

Monterisi, M. T. (2002). *Migración internacional y expansión comercial: El caso de los emigrados Lucchesi en la provincia de Córdoba.* 1880/1914. Córdoba, Argentina: Archivo Nacional.

Moraga, C. (1993). *The last generation: Prose and poetry.* Boston, MA: South End Press.

Moreno-Fraginals, M., Moya Pons, F. & Engerman, S. L. (1985). (Eds.), *Between slavery and free labor: The Spanish-speaking Caribbean in the 19th century.* Baltimore, MD: Johns Hopkins University Press.

Mullner, R. & Giachello, A. L. (2011). *Traditional health and disease beliefs, access to health care, cultural sensitivity.* Retrieved from http://www.jrank.org/cultures/pages/3951/ Health.html.

New York City Department of City Planning. (2010). *Population 2010 Demographic Tables.* Retrieved from http://www.nyc.gov/html/dcp/html/census/demo_tables_2010.shtml.

Nida, E. A. (1974). *Understanding Latin Americans: Special references to religious values and movements.* South Pasadena, CA: William Carey Library.

Noble, J. & LaCasa, J. (1991). *The Hispanic way: Aspects of behavior, attitudes, and customs of the Spanish-speaking world.* Chicago, IL: Passport Books.

Noh, S. & Kasper, V. (2003). Perceived discrimination and depression: Moderating effects of coping, acculturation, and ethnic support. *American Journal of Public Health, 93*(2), 232–239.

Novas, H. (1994). *Everything you need to know about Latino history.* New York: Plume Books.

Novas, H. (2008). *Everything you need to know about Latino history* (2nd Ed.). New York: Penguin.

Nuño, T., Dorrington, C. & Alvarez, I. (1998). *Los Angeles County Latino/Hispanic youth health assessment.* Los Angeles, CA: National Coalition of Hispanic Health and Human Services.

Otero-Carvajal, L. E. (2008). *Historia de España.* Retrieved from http://www.ucm.es/info/ hcontemp/leoc/historia%20spain.htm.

Ortiz-Cotto, F. (2011). *All countries in Latin America.* Retrieved from http://www.globalministries.org/lac/countries.

Ossio, J. (1984). Cultural continuity, structure, and context: Some peculiarities of the Andean compadrazgo. In R. T. Smith (Ed.), *Kinship ideology and practice in Latin America* (118–46). Chapel Hill, NC: University of North Carolina Press.

Pagden, A. (1986). *Letter of Hernán Cortés.* Boston, MA: Yale University Press.

Padilla, A. M. (Ed.) (1995). *Hispanic psychology: Critical issues in theory and research*. Thousand Oaks, CA.: Sage.

Papalia, D. E., Wendkos-Olds, S., Duskin-Feldman, R. & Gross, D. (2004). *Human development* (9th ed.). Boston, MA: McGraw Hill.

Pew Hispanic Center and the Kaiser Family Foundation (2002). *2002 National Survey of Latinos*. Retrieved from http://pewhispanic.org/files/reports/15.pdf.

Rodriguez, S. (1995). *Hispanics in the United States: An insight into group characteristics*. Department of Health and Human Services. Retrieved from http: //www/hhs.gov/about/heo/hgen.html.

Rodríguez-Pino, C. (1997). Teaching Spanish to native speakers: A new perspective in the 1990s. *ERIC CLL News Bulletin, 21*(1).

Rostworowski, M. (1997). *Historia de los Incas*. Lima, Peru: Prolibro, Asociación Editorial Bruño.

Rouse, I. (1993). *The Taínos: Rise and decline of the people who greeted Columbus*. Boston, MA: Yale University Press.

Ruíz-Aldea, P. (1999). *Los araucanos y sus costumbres*. (3rd ed.). Santiago, Chile: Ediciones La Ciudad.

Salmoral, M. L. (1990). *America 1492: Portrait of a continent 500 years ago*. New York and Oxford: Facts on file.

Singlis, T. M. & Brown, W. J. (1995). Culture, self, and collectivist communication: Linking culture to individual behavior. *Human Communication Research, 21*, 354–389.

Singlis, T. M., Triandis, H. C., Bhawuk, D. & Gelfand, M. J. (1995). Horizontal and vertical dimensions of individualism and collectivism: A theoretical and measurement refinement. *Cross-Cultural Research, 29*, 240–275.

Smilansky, S. (2000). *Free will and illusion*. Oxford: Oxford University Press.

Smith, J. I. (1999). *Islam in America*. New York: Columbia University Press.

Sotomayor, M. (Ed.) (1991). *Empowering Hispanic families: A critical issue for the 90s*. Milwaukee, WI: Families Intl.

Sue, D. W., Arredondo, P. & McDavis, R. J. (1992). Multicultural counseling competencies and standards: A call to the profession. *Journal of Counseling and Development, 70*, 477–486.

Taylor, J. & Turner, R. J. (2002). Perceived discrimination, social status, and depression in the transition to adulthood: Racial contrasts. *Social Psychology Quarterly, 65*(3), 213–226.

Thomas, W. & Collier, V. (1997). School effectiveness for language minority student. *NCBE Resource Collection Series, (9)*1. Washington, DC: National Clearinghouse for Bilingual Education. Retrieved from http://www.ncbe.gwu.edu/ncbepubs/resources/effectiveness/index.htm.

Triandis, H. C. & Suh, E. M. (2002). Cultural influences on personality. *Annual Review of Psychology, 53*, 133–160.

Triandis, H. C. (2001). Individualism-collectivism and personality. *Journal of Personality, 69*, 907–924.

U.S. Census Bureau. (2010). *The Hispanic population: Census 2010 brief*. Washington, DC: U.S. Government Printing Office.

U.S. Bureau of the Census (2000). Hispanic Americans today. *Current Population Reports*, 23–183. Washington, DC: U.S. Government Printing Office.

Valdés, G. (2000). Nonnative English speakers: Language bigotry in the English mainstream classrooms. *ADE Bulletin 124*. Retrieved from http//www.ade.org/ade/bulletin/N124/toc/124toc.htm.

Weller, G. (1983). The role of language as a cohesive force in the Hispanic speech community of Washington. D. C. In L. Elías-Olivares (Ed.), *Spanish in the U.S. setting: Beyond the Southwest.* National Clearinghouse for Bilingual Education. Rosslyn, VA: Inter American Research Associates.

Whybrow, P. C. (2006). *American mania: When more is not enough.* New York: W. W. Norton.

Williamson, E. (1993). *The penguin history of Latin America.* New York: Penguin.

Willis, S. L., Tennstedt, S. L., Marsiske, M., Ball, K., Elias, J., Mann-Koepke, K., Morris, J. N., Rebok, G. W., Unversagt, F. W., Stoddard, A. M. & Wright, E. (2006). Long-term effects of cognitive training on everyday functional outcomes in older adults. *American Medical Association, 296*(23), 2805–2814.

Yuen, M., Lau, P. S. Y. & Chan, R. M. C., (2000). Improving school guidance programs: A conversation with Norman C. Gysbers. *Asian Journal of Counseling, 7*(2), 19–41.

Zangwill, I. (1909). *The melting pot.* New York: Macmillan.

Zombrana, R. E. (1995). *Understanding Latino families: Scholarship, policy, and practice.* Thousands Oaks, CA: Sage.

Index

accentuation 24–6
acculturation 13–14
addictions and substances 131–4
Advanced Cognitive Training for
    Independent and Vital Elderly
    (ACTIVE) xiii
affective/emotional vocabulary 98–9
alcohol use: Alcoholics Anonymous:
    12-step program 144–5; general
    vocabulary 128–9; short- and long-term
    effects 135; short evaluation 145–6;
    slang 135
alphabet 21–2
American School Counseling Association
    (ASCA) 93
American Translators Association
    (ATA) 171
amphetamines 136–7
authority 181–2, 184

to be (ser; estar): imperfect tense 33–4;
    present tense 27; preterite 32
to become/get (poner (se)): present
    tense 29, 30
behavior/discipline vocabulary 101–4,
    119–20
bilingual charts and scales 120–1
bilingual education 94; student
    backgrounds 94–5; teaching and
    learning styles 95–6, 185
bilingual materials 169–70
bilingual populations 93–6
bilingual specialists 170–1; *see
    also* interpreters/interpreting;
    translation/translators
body language 46–7, 48, 49, 182, 183,
    184
bus transportation vocabulary 113–15

cannabinoids 131, 140–1
careers vocabulary 110–12
case studies: dreams, visions and
    voices 86–9; at the registration
    desk 54–6; substance abuse 150–60;
    suicide ideation 89–92
children as interpreters 179
classroom vocabulary 108–10
cocaine 137–8
cognitive/thoughts vocabulary 97–8
commands 69–70
communication method 184
confidentiality 171, 177, 178, 179, 181
control 185
countries 41
crisis intervention 85–92; case studies
    86–92; dreams, visions and voices 17,
    85, 86–9; medicines and home
    remedies 85–6; suicide ideation
    89–92
¿Cuál es . . . 54
cultural guidelines 184–5

dates 37–9, 121
days of the week 38
decimals 42
definite articles 49
depressants 128–9
dimensions 42
discrimination 45–6
domestic violence 75–7

emergency room 66–8
empathy 12
estar (to be): imperfect tense 33–4; present
    tense 27; preterite 32
ethical issues 177; confidentiality 171,
    177, 178, 179, 181; family in counseling

ethical issues (*cont.*):
  sessions 14–15, 179; interpreters 171,
  177, 178, 179–81; translators 171
ethnicity: diversity 4, 5; identity 4–7, 9;
  and interpreters 180; myths 7–8, 12, 13
eye contact 47, 182, 183, 184

familismo 14
family (*la familia*) 14, 184; in counseling
  sessions 14–15, 179; names 121
to feel (sentir (se)): present tense 30;
  preterite 31
formalities and etiquette 18, 46, 182–3, 184
fractions 41

gender 180, 184; *see also hembrismo;
  machismo*
gestures 48, 49
greetings 46–7, 184

hallucinogenic drugs 130; LSD 141–2;
  PCP 143–4
to have (tener): imperfect tense 33–4;
  present tense 28; preterite 32
hembrismo 16
heroin 138–9
Hispanics *see* Latinos/Hispanics
home remedies 85–6

identity 4–7, 9
imperfect tense: irregular verbs 33–4;
  regular verbs 32–3
inhalants 139–40
intake interview 56–7; in-depth life
  history questionnaire 57–63; with
  interpreter 177–9
interpreters/interpreting 171; concurrent
  vs. sequential translation 176; ethical
  issues 171, 177, 178, 179–81; linguistic
  diversity 180–1; proficiency and
  qualifications 171–5, 180–1; rules for
  interpretation 175–7; techniques
  177–9, 178*f*; time and pace 177

language acquisition xii–xiii, 19–21
Latinos/Hispanics: demographic
  profiles 9*f*, 10*f*, 10*t*, 11*t*, 12*f*;
  discrimination 45–6; ethnic myths 7–8,
  12, 13; history 3–4, 10; identity 4–7,
  9; linguistic diversity 3–4, 8, 180–1;
  origins 3; racial and ethnic diversity 4,
  5; terminology 7, 8; in the United
  States 1–2

learning and teaching styles 95–6, 185
legal status 71
lethality assessment 78
life history questionnaire 57–63
lifestyle 162; enjoyable and gratifying
  activities 162–5; problem-solving
  skills 167; social skills 165–6
linguistic diversity 3–4, 8, 180–1
LSD 141–2

machismo 15–16, 180
Marianismo 16
marijuana 140–1
medical terms 63–71; commands 69–70;
  emergency room vocabulary 66–8;
  identifying somatic symptoms 63–6,
  70–1; parts of the body 63–5;
  questions 70–1; similar in English and
  Spanish 65–6; useful phrases 68–9
medicines and home remedies 85–6
mind, body, and spirit 17, 85, 86–9, 185
modesty 183
months of the year 37–8
mood disorders 74
multicultural counseling competencies 9;
  developing sensitivity and empathy 12;
  eradication of ethnic myths 12;
  knowledge-base and understanding of
  background 10
multiculturalism 94
multilingualism 94

names 47, 121
nationalities 41
Necesita . . . 52–3
Necesito . . . 53
nicotine 142–3
non-verbal communication 181;
  body language 46–7, 48, 49, 182,
  183, 184; modesty, privacy, dress,
  appearance 183; personal space 182–3;
  submission to authority 181–2, 184
numbers 34; cardinal numbers 34–6;
  ordinal numbers 37

occupational choices vocabulary 110–12
opioid drugs 130, 138–9
orientation 184

parents: interviews 121–4;
  vocabulary 112–13
parts of the body 63–5
past tenses 30–4

patriarcalismo (patriarchalism) 16–17, 181–2
PCP 143–4
personal space 182–3
pharmacological drugs 131
poner (se) (to become/get): present tense 29, 30
post-traumatic stress disorder 75
present tense: *to be (ser; estar)* 27; irregular verbs 28–30; regular verbs 27–8
preterite 30; irregular verbs 32; regular verbs 31
problem-solving skills 167
psychological symptoms 71–8; cultural norms 78; domestic violence 75–7; general questions 77–8; key words 71–2; mood disorders 74; post-traumatic stress disorder 75; psychosocial stress 74–5; psychotic disorders 73; schizophrenia 73
psychomotor/behavioral vocabulary 99–100
psychosocial stress 74–5
psychotic disorders 73

questionnaires: in-depth life history questionnaire 57–63; substance abuse history 146–50
questions: basic questions 42–3, 50–2; psychological symptoms 77–8; at registration 50–2; somatic symptoms 70–1

reader's companion website 18, 21, 57, 71, 178
reading comprehension and language vocabulary 116–18
registering at reception 46–56; basic dialogues 54–6; first contact 46; greetings 46–7, 184; names 47, 121; questions and expressions 50–2; useful nouns 48–9; useful verbs 49–50
religion 16, 17
respect 46, 47, 95–6, 182

schizophrenia 73
school cafeteria vocabulary 113–15
school counselors/psychologists 93–124; affective/emotional domain 98–9; bilingual charts and scales 120–1; bilingual eduation 94–6; bilingual populations 93–6; bilingual specialists 170–1; bus transportation

vocabulary 113–15; careers and occupational choices 110–12; classroom vocabulary 108–10; cognitive/thoughts domain 97–8; general school vocabulary 96–7; homework vocabulary 112–13; learning and teaching styles 95–6, 185; lunch and school cafeteria 113–15; parents meetings 112–13, 121–4; psychomotor/behavioral domain 99–100; reading comprehension and language 116–18; report cards 112–13; special needs students 104–8; students' backgrounds 94–5; students' behavior 101–4; typical consequences of bad behavior 103–4
school psychology 118–20; disruptive behavior/externalising problems 119–20; DSM-IV-TR vocabulary 118–20
seasons of the year 38
sensitivity 12, 14–15, 47, 185
sentir (se) (to feel): present tense 30; preterite 31
ser (to be): imperfect tense 33–4; present tense 27; preterite 32
social skills 165–6
socioeconomic status 183
somatic symptoms 63–6, 70–1
Spanish xiii; accentuation 24–6; alphabet 21–2; basic questions 42–3, 50–2; broadcast/generic Spanish xiii–xiv; countries and nationalities 41; date/time vocabulary 37–40, 121; definite articles 49; fractions, decimals and dimensions 41–2; general vocabulary similar to English 22–4; greetings 46–7; language acquisition tips 19–21; months, days and seasons 37–8; numbers 34–7; past tenses 30–4; present tense 27–30
Spanish materials 169–70
special needs students 104–8
spirituality 17, 85, 86–9, 185
stimulants 130; amphetamines 136–7; cocaine 137–8; nicotine 142–3
substance abuse 125–67; abuse-related vocabulary 128; addictions and substances 131–4; alcohol 128–9, 135, 144–6; cannabinoids 131, 140–1; case studies 150–60; depressants 128–9; hallucinogenic drugs 130, 141–4; history questionnaire 146–50;

substance abuse (*cont.*):
  interviews and interventions 144–62;
  lifestyle strategies 162–7; opioid
  drugs 130, 138–9; pharmacological
  drugs 131; planning treatment
  phrases 161–2; short- and long-term
  effects 134–44; stimulants 130, 136–8,
  142–3; terminology and concepts
  125–34; verbs similar in English and
  Spanish 126–8
suicide risk evaluation 78–85; case
  study 89–92; danger to himself/
  herself 78–81, 83–4; danger to
  others 81–3, 84; general and final
  evaluation 83; summary 84–5

tener (to have): imperfect tense 33–4;
  present tense 28; preterite 32
¿Tiene . . . 54
Tiene que . . . 53
time: cultural view of 184;
  expressions 38–40
translation/translators 169–70;
  ethical issues 171; proficiency and
  qualifications 170–5

verbs: imperfect tense 32–4; past
  tenses 30–4; present tense 27–30;
  preterite 30–2
voice: hearing voices 86–9; volume 48,
  179–80